VICTORIAN COSTUME

VICTORIAN COSTUME
AND
COSTUME ACCESSORIES

ANNE BUCK

REVISED SECOND EDITION

RUTH BEAN
CARLTON BEDFORD
1984

Originally published by Herbert Jenkins, London 1961
This edition published by
Ruth Bean Publishers, Carlton, Bedford MK43 7LP. England

ISBN   0 903585 17 0

Cover photograph: By courtesy of Manchester City Galleries

The Bromley family by Ford Madox Brown, 1844
*The bodice shaping of the 1840s is clear in the dress on the right, with the
sleeves now beginning to open at the wrist to show the undersleeves.
The three younger women all wear deep, falling collars of lace at the low,
v-shaped neckline. The dress, hairdressing and elaborate cap of the
older woman is still in the fashion of the late 1830s. The men wear coats
showing the slit cuff of the 1840s and early 1850s and one shows a shirt
with button or stud fastening below his dark cravat.*

Printed in Great Britain at the University Press, Cambridge

FOREWORD TO SECOND EDITION

The text has been reprinted without alteration from the first edition, but there are additional illustrations showing details of textiles and construction and a more spacious grouping of some items for clearer presentation. All illustrations now appear within the relevant chapter. A new section has been added to the bibliography of publications issued since the first edition of 1961.

I am most grateful to Miss Jane Tozer and Miss Sarah Levitt, Keeper and Assistant Keeper, Gallery of English Costume, Platt Hall, Manchester for all their help in providing the new illustrations and to Mr Mark Cobley, the City Art Galleries photographer. I am also much indebted to Mrs Ruth Bean for her enthusiasm in undertaking a new edition of this book and for her skill and care in producing it.

Anne Buck   March 1984

PREFACE

By

HUGH WAKEFIELD

Keeper of the Department of Circulation, Victoria and Albert Museum

THE interest of collectors is being drawn increasingly towards the decorative arts of the Victorian period. Sufficient time has now elapsed since Queen Victoria's death for the arts of her reign to be seen in true perspective. They can be judged for their intrinsic interest and for their beauty; they are no longer merely old-fashioned.

The history of Victorian art in its many forms is exceedingly complex, and needs to be approached with careful discrimination. The books in this series represent a serious attempt on the part of the Editor and the various authors to present information which is based firmly upon the study of Victorian objects and contemporary accounts of them, rather than upon the uncertainties of secondary sources.

Miss Anne Buck, B.A., F.M.A., has been Keeper of the Gallery of English Costume at Platt Hall, Manchester, since 1947. In this capacity she has been largely responsible for the development of the important collection there, and she has drawn on it extensively to provide the illustrations for this book. Besides describing Victorian dress fashions in detail, she has paid close attention to the costume accessories which were characteristic of the period. New information of this sort will be of value not merely to collectors of costume and of fashion plates, but also to students of dress design and to all those who need to use costume as a means of dating the other Victorian arts.

AUTHOR'S PREFACE

THE Victorian age still stands so solid and enduring around us that we hardly realize how much of it is disappearing from our sight. We see its architecture everywhere in our cities. We have been brought up on its literature, its history, its politics. We know it as an age which poured out volumes of the written and printed word and which invented the photograph to make exact and permanent record of its transient scenes. We think we know enough about it, or at least have enough evidence somewhere for all we could ever want to know about it. But it is not only in the massive Town Hall, in the revelations of parliamentary reports, that we see the Victorian age. In the Victorian sideboard, the Victorian muffin-dish, the Victorian scrapbook, the age has also left its individual mark, a fragment of it has been caught. An age of great possessions, it left many such things behind it and, because of their very abundance, we have been careless of them and of their gradual disappearance.

Amongst the material possessions left behind by the Victorians are some of the clothes they wore and objects, useful or decorative, that they wore or carried about with them. Such things take us as close as we can now get to the living presence of that age. Yet the dress itself worn once by the living bodies of men and women has one great discouragement for the collector. Most collectors demand that the objects of their search shall please the eye, or shall at least be objects complete and satisfying in themselves. A chair, a silver candlestick, a wineglass, discovered in a house, in a dealer's showroom, in a saleroom, each appears now to the collecting eye exactly as it did in the house in which it was first used. A Victorian dress, found hanging forgotten in a wardrobe, separated for ever from the body which once gave it form, does not. Nor can we restore this form completely by anything so simple as putting the dress on a living body of our own time. In discovering this, however, we discover in the empty dress a new interest. This is the mould which its age fashioned, which it imposed on the living form.

The true form of the dress is not at once apparent when we pick it up now, because it lacks, first of all, the support and shaping once given to it by the human form, the human form of its own time; it lacks, secondly, the reinforcing forms of corset, bustle, crinoline and underwear proper and necessary to it. Dress is a composite achievement. The dress gives the final appearance but it is not the dress alone which can produce it. There can be no understanding of Victorian costume, or costume of any period, without some knowledge of its underlying structure. Fashion plates give the changing outlines, the decorative details in line, but the connection of a dress of the 1860s, as it appears when rediscovered now in a box or drawer, with one of the exquisite toilettes of a plate in *La Mode Illustrée*, or even the less elegant *Englishwoman's Domestic Magazine*, is not at once apparent.

Fashion plates are the sensitive record of fashion changes, but much of the detail, the lesser changes, the extravagancies, reached only a small proportion of Victorian costume. Throughout the whole period, almost all the fashion plates are of French origin and the number of women in this country who dressed like the fashion plates and followed their slightest changes was always very small. But sometimes, even in fashion plates, the years pass and there seems to be little alteration in the main form, even in the details of dress. There are periods—for example 1840 to 1845—when the fashions which are announced month by month in the fashion notes of journals bring little real change even at the highest level of fashion. Fashion writing has a language of its own and must always be read with care. It must be checked with the illustrations which accompany it, with the fashion of the moment, and the moment which has just passed, always in mind. We read, perhaps, that gloves are long, but find that the engraving shows the same wrist-length style that has been the fashion for several years: the change is one from one inch above the wrist to two. This may be the beginning of a new style, of a change which will ultimately bring the glove to the elbow again, but it may be only a slight variation in shortness. At other times, for example during the 1870s, each year is significant, giving slight but perceptible movement to the change which sharply divides the dress of 1874 from the dress of 1876.

At a fashionable level it should be possible to distinguish a dress of 1874 from one of 1876 from outline alone, but a knowledge of the outlines of the changing styles which are Victorian costume is not always enough, nor are all surviving dresses of the highest fashion. The way a dress fastens may be a more certain guide to its date than its general line. Any theatrical costumier can make a dress which will pass in appearance as a dress of the year of Queen Victoria's accession; but it is very unlikely that any dress made outside the first few years of the reign will have its sleeves set as low on the arm as was the fashion then, or the seams of the bodice so meticulously piped. Silver bears by law the hall-mark of its year; but for every period there are unconscious hall-marks of decoration and construction. In dress, details of fabric, pattern, colour, ornament and technical devices, which flourish for a few years and then disappear, stamp it with the mark of those years. Some details may appear again a decade or a generation later, but they never reappear exactly as before.

CONTENTS

LIST OF PLATES

LIST OF LINE ILLUSTRATIONS

ACKNOWLEDGEMENTS TO FIRST EDITION

MY thanks are due, in the first place, to Manchester City Art Galleries, who in 1947 established a Gallery of English Costume at Platt Hall. What I have learned from the day-to-day care and handling of this collection is the real basis of this book.

I am glad also to have this opportunity of thanking colleagues in many other museums who have made their collections available for examination, and have from time to time given help and information from their own studies. I owe an early debt to the pioneer work of Miss Thalassa Cruso at the London Museum. This museum's catalogue published in 1935 is still the only attempt at a catalogue of a costume collection and includes one of the best brief historical summaries available.

I am, of course, indebted to many other published works, particularly such recent studies as John Irwin's *Shawls* and Norah Waugh's *Corsets and Crinolines*. No one can now write on Victorian costume without owing much to Dr. C. Willett Cunnington's *Englishwomen's Clothing in the Nineteenth Century*. My own writing on men's costume in the present book has benefited from his work (with Phillis Cunnington), *Handbook of English Costume in the Nineteenth Century*. My debt to Dr. and Mrs. Cunnington is, however, more than a debt to their books, and I should like to acknowledge here the generous help I have always had from them.

In the preparation of this book I have had much help at every stage from Miss Zillah Halls, until recently my colleague at the Gallery of English Costume, and from Mr. Hugh Wakefield, the Editor of the series.

I am indebted to the Manchester City Art Galleries for permission to reproduce all the plates in this book which are not individually acknowledged to other sources. The other sources are The Tate Gallery, London (Plates 3 and 6); The Walker Art Gallery, Liverpool (Plate 2); The City Museum and Art Gallery, Birmingham (Plate 5); to whom I offer my thanks.

I have acknowledged individually the source of the various line drawings which illustrate the text. To the publishers of the journals in which these drawings originally appeared I also offer thanks.

ANNE BUCK

CHAPTER 1

DRESSES — 1837-50

VICTORIAN dress was a sequence of many different styles. Each evolved gradually from the one before and emerged at last, sharp and definite, as a new form. This first phase of each new style gave the new lines clearly, without adornment. Then there was an elaboration, a blurring of this line in ornament and detail; in this the next style began to shape itself and emerged in its turn, a new fashion from the old. But the process was always continuous and there was never a sharp break between old and new.

The emergence of the early Victorian style, the first style of the reign, coincided almost exactly with the Queen's accession. It had been shaped between 1834 and 1836, and by 1837 the line was set firmly for the next twenty years. It showed development, variation and elaboration but no major change. The line was already set in 1837 though it had not yet reached its climax. The bodice had downward curving lines at the shoulder, repeated in the lines of the curving, pointed waistline. Beneath this, the skirt curved over the hips, falling to a wide hemline. During the 1840s this tapering bodice-form lengthened, bringing the waist as low as possible. All lines of construction, all lines of ornament, on the bodice concentrated on carrying the eye to the pointed waistline, emphasizing—even creating—the slender waist which was the fashionable ideal of the time. Beneath it, the skirt curved out with increasing fullness. These plain, clean lines of the 1840s mark the climax of the first style of the reign. The ornament is part of the line, emphasizing yet subdued to it (Plate 1).

The date of a dress from the opening of the reign to about 1850 is revealed partly by the level of the waistline—before 1840 it was slightly above the natural level, after 1840 it fell steadily—and partly by the increasing width of the skirt. There is great variation in skirt width, but generally only a small proportion of dresses

19

before 1845 have a hem-width greater than four yards; after 1845 a width of between four and five yards is general. In day dresses there is another, even more distinguishing, mark of date. This is the sleeve. A dress with a full sleeve is likely to be a dress of 1835 or earlier. In that year the fullness started to disappear and by 1837 the tight sleeve was completely established. "I hope you who are so fashionable a person have already made all your sleeves quite tight to your arm—but the question is useless for I know you will not think of going out with such an old-fashioned thing as a full sleeve at present" (*Cecilia: The Life and Letters of Cecilia Ridley, 1819–45* (1958), May 1837). Amongst the unfashionable, the transitional stage, with the sleeve still cut full but the fullness gathered in close to the arm above the elbow and moderate fullness in the lower half, was probably worn for a year or two longer By 1840, even at a less fashionable level, the sleeve fitted closely. Then by 1844 it began to widen and open at the wrist. In evening dress the sleeve was short and tight throughout this first period.

The evening neckline was low, excessively low: "far too much so for strict delicacy to approve" (*Ladies Cabinet*, 1844). It made a horizontal line, low on the shoulders, or curved to a slight point at the centre. The fashion of trimming this neckline with flat folds of the fabric of the dress continued from the early 1830s. This ornament may be found on evening dresses throughout the 1840s (Plate 1); but after 1843 a plain neckline, with the addition of deep falling collars of lace, became increasingly fashionable.

Before 1840 a low neckline was still often worn with day dress, and continued for more formal day dress into the early 1840s. A bodice with a fairly high round neck, the back particularly high, became more general in the 1840s. Back-fastening was general for all bodices of the period. Bodice fronts were often trimmed with pinked frills of the material of the dress, which passed from the shoulder, following the line of the bodice shaping to the waist, forming a deep V-shape and emphasizing this dominant line of the dress. This trimming was often called pelerine lapels, pelerine lapels *en cœur*, or heart pelerine bodice. An alternative form has the bodice front open at the neck to reveal a white chemisette worn beneath. From 1843 into the 1850s, some dresses have a loose panel, pleated into the shoulders and gathered together at the centre waist, which formed a fan shape over the front of the bodice, still emphasizing its tapering lines. This style is more often found in surviving dresses and in photographs than in fashion plates. After 1846, bodices with basques began to appear, the first stage of the new jacket bodice with basques which is the main style of the 1850s. The pelisse, or coat, form of dress which is often mentioned in fashion notes of the 1840s and often appears in fashion plates, is rarely found amongst surviving dresses.

The bodices were mostly cut with a centre front seam and shaped by a dart each side of it. There were usually three bones in front, one along the centre seam and one along each dart; there was also a short one at each side seam and sometimes a boned back fastening (Plate 12). But not all dresses have this full array of boning. All bodices were lined, usually with cotton; but the lining of some of the more elaborate dresses was of silk. Sometimes padding was inserted to provide an adequate curve for the bust, placed well up towards the arm. The fastening at the back was usually with hooks and eyelet holes or hooks and metal eyes. The lining sometimes had a separate fastening. The seams of the bodices were piped, particularly in the first years of the period, often in double piping in two colours to match the main shades of the dress. Piping was less conspicuously used after 1845, but might still reinforce edges and main seams.

The dresses of this first period are almost all one-piece dresses with bodice and skirt joined, except a few which are made with two bodices, a long-sleeved, high bodice for day and a short-sleeved, low-necked bodice for evening. The manner of joining is a guide to date and is also an important factor in the development of the 1840s line. At the beginning of the period, skirts were set on the bodice in flat pleats, or in gathers if the fabric was muslin, with gathers at the centre back. From 1841, as the skirts grew wider, a new method of setting the skirt appeared "by gauging it all round the top as far as the points of the hips; by this means that excessive fullness which would be otherwise disposed of in gathers or pleats is formed exactly to the shape, but on the other hand this method lengthens the waist excessively and gives an air of stiffness to the figure" (*World of Fashion*, 1841). The fabric, with its lining, was closely pleated and sewn to the bodice at each alternate fold (Plate 12). This method was used on dresses until the end of the decade. Skirts were always lined, except in dresses of cotton, muslin or net. Their usual lining was a glazed cotton. From the mid-1840s, a narrow woollen braid was generally added to the hem to take the wear off the lower edge of the dress. A pocket in the lining of the skirt, rare before 1840, was often inserted in dresses of the late 1840s. Skirts were usually plain in line; but, from 1843, evening dresses with two or three skirts were worn, which gave the effect of two or three deep flounces. By the end of the decade, flounced skirts had become the general form for day and evening wear.

The dress of the early Victorian period romantically revived details of line and garments from the dress of earlier periods. The low neckline with the deep collar of lace was the neckline of the seventeenth century. The long mantles with scarf ends when made in black silk recall the cloaks of this form which were worn during the eighteenth century. The silks which were used for evening wear between 1835 and 1845 include brocaded silks, richly flowered, like those of the eighteenth century. Some of these were based on earlier patterns and are not always easy to distinguish from an eighteenth-century fabric. Confusion with the eighteenth century is increased because, under the influence of this fashion, economical women of the late 1830s and early 1840s who could lay hands on an eighteenth-century dress had it remade in the fashion of their own day. Enough of these renovations survive in museum collections to show that the making up of dresses in the styles of 1835 to 1845 from eighteenth-century silk was a not uncommon practice. How much they were worn is another matter. Some reveal themselves by not being very successful, even by being left half-done; others betray an earlier existence only by a few tell-tale pieces remaining from it. Many other silks were also worn for evening dress, particularly satin, and watered silk, plain or with satin stripe. Velvet, often mentioned in the fashion journals, was either of more limited use or has less often survived. Most characteristic of all the silks of the 1840s, and the most characteristic fabric of the decade, was "changeable", shot or glacé silk, plain or figured, with delicate and subtle shadings of colour into colour. This silk was used for day dresses as well as evening wear. Silks were becoming more generally worn in day dresses by 1840, taking the place of the printed muslins of the 1820s and early 1830s.

Challis, a mixed fabric of silk warp and fine worsted weft, was much used for dresses between 1830 and 1840 and is one of the most characteristic fabrics of this decade. It was sometimes woven with a satin stripe and was usually printed in colours on its natural cream ground. It was mainly a fabric for day dresses but was also used for less formal evening dress. It became less fashionable after 1840, but other mixed fabrics, silk and wool, wool and cotton, with woven or printed designs are found among the dresses of the 1840s. Very fine woollen materials, light and open in weave, were often used. These also often had printed patterns.

By 1840 printed muslins had lost the fashionable incentive of the 1820s and 1830s and appear less in the dresses of the 1840s than in those of the 1830s. Clear white muslin was popular as a summer fabric and for youthful evening wear.

Unlike the shot silks with their soft, luminous colourings, the printed woollen fabrics of the time often show bright and richly mixed colours (Plate 15). The contrast of black with bright and light colours was popular in the 1830s, particularly in the middle years of the decade. Brightly coloured patterns on a dark ground appeared in fabrics. Black satin aprons and black mantles were worn over bright dresses, and black was fashionable for bonnet veils and mittens. The colourings of the 1840s are generally less rich and exuberant, except in the printed woollen fabrics and the shawls, but the contrast of black lace and light satins for evening wear was still fashionable in the 1840s. Dark green, and shades of blue, pink and mauve were much worn all through the 1840s, and the mingling of colour in the shot silks has left a great range of soft and opalescent shades.

The patterns, both printed and woven, had less exuberance than those of the 1830s. The fashionable shawl patterns influenced many designs, particularly in printed woollen fabrics (Plate 15). Printed muslins, now less fashionable, often had small sprigged patterns closely printed over the ground. The woven patterns of silks, apart from those following the eighteenth-century tradition, were usually floral patterns, often showing only a single flower or leaf form, but flowing closely and freely over the ground (Plate 15). Striped silks and checkered silks were also worn, as well as a great deal of plain silk.

The lack of added ornament is an outstanding characteristic of the dress of the 1840s. The contrast of the texture of velvet ribbon in a shade toning with the silk of the dress was fashionable throughout the decade. It was applied in bands round the widening sleeve opening and on the skirt. The skirt ornament was usually shaped in an inverted V from waist to hem, but a central line of ornament, and ornament down one side, are also found. Sometimes a light braid was used and, after 1846, fringe trimmings began to appear. The evening dresses were softened and enriched by trimmings of lace, which may not always survive with them.

Some of the deep falling collars of lace worn with evening dresses of the 1840s were a single straight flounce of lace, but others were made up from several narrower laces, mounted on net and trimmed with ribbons. Most of them are in the bobbin laces of the time, particularly blonde, the fragile silk bobbin lace; but others are of the machine-made lace which was being increasingly used by the 1840s. Pelerines or deep collars of lace, net or muslin were also worn in the 1840s over day dresses. Some are rounded at the back with a V-shaped front, others are V-shaped back and front. The pelerines of the early 1830s, which are more often of embroidered muslin, are wide over the shoulders, making a horizontal line across the back, and usually have short ends extending below the waist in front.

The large square collars of embroidered muslin which were also worn with the dresses of the 1830s were just passing out of fashion in 1837 with the changing line of the dress. "Large ones are now quite out of fashion in outdoor dress; we see only the sharp pointed collars that wrap across and fasten with a brooch or else the little round collars. The most elegant are embroidered in rich but light patterns and finished at the edge with Valenciennes lace" (*World of Fashion*, 1837). The collar remained small, not only through the 1840s but also during the 1850s and 1860s (Fig. 1). With the open front of some dresses a chemisette was worn, often with a small round collar attached.

When the sleeve widened at the wrist in the second half of the

1840s, short undersleeves of muslin, net or lace were worn. These differ from the later undersleeves by being short, extending only half-way from the wrist to the elbow. There are also frilled cuffs, usually in the form of an insertion of lace or muslin with a frill each side, which were worn over tight sleeves.

All these additions to a dress of the 1840s may be of embroidered muslin, muslin and lace, or net and lace. The embroidery in raised satin stitch (see page 172) on white muslin, which enriched

FIGURE 1.—EMBROIDERED MUSLIN COLLAR (*Lady's Newspaper, 1851*)
Embroidery on muslin in cotton in raised satin stitch, the edge in button-hole stitch and the spaces between the embroidery filled with lacework stitches.

much of the dress of the 1830s, still appeared on the smaller areas of these chemisettes and collars (Fig. 1), but there was a tendency for the embroidery to become more mechanical and less delicate towards the middle of the century. Small collars in fine knitting and beaded mesh were also used.

A characteristic addition at the neck of dresses for this early period was a neck knot or neck tie. There were several kinds. At the opening of the period "A fraise has replaced neck knots, collarettes—cravats of all kinds" (*Court Magazine*, 1836). The fraise was muslin half an ell long and an eighth of an ell wide (22½ in. by 5½ in.), embroidered and trimmed with a ruche, folded

across in fichu style and fastened with a large ornamental pin.
There were also small scarves for cravats "tied negligently".
Throughout the 1840s, ties of silk and velvet ribbon were worn,
crossed and held by a brooch or pin. The ribbon was usually
narrow, not more than an inch wide, and about twenty inches
long, and might be plain, figured or embroidered.

CHAPTER 2

DRESSES — 1850-65

THE first phase of Victorian dress ends about 1850. The change which came then was a change in character, a new emphasis to the developing style, rather than a new style. Flounces on the skirt spread it out into ever-widening circles. The sleeve opened at the wrist over full undersleeves of lace or muslin. The patterned flounces and the details of bodice trimming gave a new horizontal emphasis to the line of the dress. The loosening of the bodice in a jacket form with basques softened and loosened this line. Even in its plainer versions, this second Victorian style is a softer, more decorated version of the first

Bodices with basques and "Corsages forming a kind of waist-coat" (*World of Fashion*, 1846) were appearing as early as 1846, and by 1851 the jacket bodice was established as an alternative form to the back fastening bodice of day dress. "Those which are of the basque or jacket form are greatly in favour" (*World of Fashion*, 1851). It remained the prevailing style for all dress except evening dress until 1859, although the back-fastening form and the back-fastening form with basques simulating a jacket, are still found on dresses of the 1850s. The jacket was either high to the neck or with a V-shaped opening with a chemisette worn beneath.

The sleeves of all bodices for day wear in the 1850s show a steadily increasing width at the opening. The widening sleeve repeated on a smaller scale the widening form of the skirt. This opened sleeve was made and trimmed in several different ways during the decade, but was generally a version of the form called the pagoda sleeve, which from a narrow upper arm spread to a wide opening (Plates 3 and 4). In 1857, very wide open sleeves appeared, made from a square of material pleated into the arm-hole and hanging wide and open from it. By 1860, the pagoda sleeve was passing out of fashion, but it still continued to be worn in the early 1860s. A closed, but full sleeve, the bishop sleeve, had begun to appear as an alternative from 1855; another version of this, with a series of puffs down the arm, also appeared in the late 1850s. Just after 1860, the bishop sleeve flattened into a sleeve shaped for the elbow, with an inner and an outer seam, a sleeve full but with only a two-dimensional fullness. Just before and just after 1860, all these different forms might be found, but the last development was the most general sleeve shape of the mid-1860s. Epaulettes appeared, often emphasized by trimming, at the top of many sleeves from 1858.

In the wearing of the jacket bodice, the waistline, which had been outlined and emphasized with so much care in the dresses

FIGURE 2.—BERTHES (*Lady's Newspaper. 1851*)
(*Left*) Net drawn up with four narrow coloured ribbons above a deep fall of lace, long-ended ribbon bow; (*Right*) Brussels lace on shaped foundation of tulle and long-ended bow of ribbon.

of the 1840s, showed less clearly; and when, by 1859, a new bodice began to replace the jacket bodice, it showed a new waistline at a new, higher level. In some dresses of the early 1860s the line still showed a slight pointing at the front; in others it ended in a straight line. These usually had belts of the same material. This new bodice kept the front fastening of the jacket.

The change in evening bodices was less than in day bodices. They were still fitting, with long, pointed waistline and back fastening. Unlike the bodices of the 1840s, they sometimes—from 1856—had a point at the back as well as the front. The neckline remained very low, forming a wide shallow curve over the shoulders. Its ornament was a softer and complex drapery of net, lace, ribbon or flowers (Fig. 2). A narrow edging of lace, net or muslin was often sewn inside the top of the bodice, and, drawn up with a narrow ribbon, showed an inch or so above the neck drapery. This is not found in dresses of the 1840s. Sleeves were very short and slightly puffed.

Bodices continued to be lined, boned and, if necessary, padded. The boning of day bodices changed in the jacket bodice, which was sometimes boned at the side seams; if it had boning in front, two short bones were inserted rather close together on each side of the front opening. This boning continued in the front-fastening bodices of the early 1860s. It is shorter and lighter than the boning of the 1840s. Jacket bodices were usually made with three shaped sections at the back, continuous with the basque, but some have horizontal darts giving the appearance of a seam, and a few actually have a seam. The evening bodices with back fastening keep the longer bones, three or five meeting at the centre front, one at each side, and boning at the back opening. There are many examples of dresses with two bodices, one for day, one for evening from this period.

The change to a jacket bodice meant that separate bodice and skirt were worn. The fullness of the skirt was set into a waistband, usually in a series of flat double box-pleats, with or without a narrow section of gathering at the back. The muslins and the light unlined materials were gathered. The short front-fastening bodice, which appeared at the end of the 1850s and was worn throughout the 1860s, was often attached to the skirt, but the skirt fullness was generally held by a waistband and not set directly on to the bodice as in the 1840s.

The width of the skirt during the early 1850s was supported by petticoats in great number, variety and weight. Half-way through the decade, a device of the eighteenth century was revived and the skirt was given a supporting framework. The crinoline frame was first a petticoat distended by whalebone hoops sewn into it, but developed into a light structure of covered steel wire (Fig. 3). The frame was given the name crinoline from the horsehair petticoat which it superseded. The wearing of it changed the line of the skirt, giving it a round, domelike form in the 1850s. After 1860 the dome flattened a little in front, a shaping which continued until the crinoline became a half-crinoline only in the

late 1860s. This framework gave a lightness and a sometimes un-
manageable buoyancy to the dress (Plate 5). The different shaping
of the crinoline frame which came about 1860 went with a new
shaping of the material of the skirt.

The skirts of the dresses of the 1850s were often flounced. The
flounces gave added fullness to the skirt without adding more
material at the waist. They softened its line and emphasized its
width by their pattern. The flounces were usually "à disposition",
that is, woven, printed or, sometimes, embroidered as flounces
so that bands of pattern lay across the width of the skirt. Flounces
of this kind were a fashion of 1851 to 1860 (Plates 3 and 4). They
began to disappear from the skirts of day dresses by 1857, when

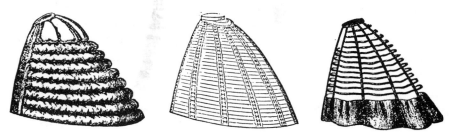

FIGURE 3.—CRINOLINES (*Queen, 1864*)
(*Left*) Petticoat of puffed horsehair in white or grey; (*Centre*) The "Sans-
flectum" crinoline; (*Right*) The "Ondina" or waved crinoline.

the crinoline frame was established, and the skirts, as wide now
without their flounces as they had been before with them, spread
without ornament over it. By 1860 the hem was emphasized by
a band of ornament (Plate 21) or sometimes still by a band of
flouncing. "The reign of crinoline is not yet over, although it is
doubtful whether the fashion will last more than a few months
longer; certain it is that to show to advantage the present style
of dress, which is very full and long and trimmed so much at the
bottom, a great amplitude of underskirt is required" (*Englishwoman's Domestic Magazine*, 1860). The fashion lasted not only a
few months, but a few years longer. From 1860 the skirts were
cut with some gored sections, to achieve greater fullness at the
hem without increasing it at the waist. The skirts of the early

1860s usually have a plain width at the front with gored sections each side. Some have a plain width at the back and often plain widths each side, amongst the gored sections. The straight edge of each gored section is always to the front of the dress. This gives the skirt the shape which is also given in the crinoline frame from this date, the slightly flattened front with the fullness sweeping to the back. The skirt was pleated on to the waistband with a short, plain section, pleated each side, at the front. The separate skirts of the 1850s dresses with jacket bodices fasten at the back. The skirts of the 1860s, whether their bodice is attached or not, fasten on the left side at the front. A pocket in the side seam was very usual in dresses of the early 1850s and was often included in silk dresses of the late 1850s and early 1860s. During the 1850s a small pocket for a watch was often made at the waist of the dress, a fashion which continued throughout the 1860s. A narrow woollen braid continued to be added at the hem of walking dresses to protect the edge from wear. The hemline itself was sometimes shaped in scallops in the mid-1860s. From the mid-1850s, while the crinoline frame was being worn, some silk dresses were made without lining to the skirt. Others have a lighter, but stiffer lining, of stiffened muslin, instead of the glazed cotton of the earlier period. But many examples show the continued use of this earlier type of lining.

Some of the skirts of day dresses of the 1860s have inside them an arrangement of rings and cords along the hem. These were for lifting up the skirt of the dress. The cord was manipulated at the waist and the skirt rose in gathered-up drapery several inches from the ground, revealing the ankles or a brightly coloured petticoat, specially worn for this purpose. In the early 1850s a lady from America, Mrs. Amelia Bloomer, tried to introduce a form of dress with full trousers visible beneath a tunic dress. This brave attempt was at once the butt of caricature and satire, although there is little other evidence to suggest that Mrs. Bloomer's costume ever became a fashion in England. No example of it has yet come to light. It was not until the 1890s, when cycling became popular, that some women wore knickerbockers visibly as part of cycling dress.

Amongst the dresses of the 1860s there are also signs of the beginning of a new form. These are the matching skirts and jackets or skirts and capes which were worn, with a white bodice or chemisette, usually as seaside or country wear. This costume is one of the forerunners of an important development in women's dress, the tailor-made coat and skirt, worn with a blouse, which came at the end of the century. The skirts and jackets, or capes, were usually made in light woollen fabric, linen or cotton piqué. A broad belt was often worn at the junction of skirt and bodice. The Swiss belt in silk or velvet was often used. This was a broad belt shaped to a double point at back and front, about four inches wide at the waist point, a characteristic and popular accessory of the early 1860s. The white bodice was also worn with a coloured skirt as an indoor costume, with or without a jacket, so that already in the 1860s there was a fashion for wearing a blouse and skirt as informal wear. The blouse, however, was not yet so called, but was known as a bodice, chemisette, or canezou (Fig. 4). The Garibaldi shirt or bodice was popular amongst these informal bodices of the early 1860s (Fig. 5). It was inspired by Garibaldi's red shirt and, in its earlier forms in 1861, it was a loose bodice of red cashmere with front fastening and bands on the shoulder. But it became so popular that many other versions of it appeared in white cambric, with or without a belt. Garibaldi jackets as well as bodices were also worn between 1860 and 1865. This informal dress rarely appears in museum displays, because its parts have often become separated.

The silks with flounces woven *à disposition* were a characteristic fabric of the 1850s. They were made to match the material of the dress, and often narrow frills showing the same pattern on a smaller scale were used for the bodice trimming. In the early 1850s, their patterns, woven or printed, tended to be floral and elaborate; later they were often in plainer, horizontally-striped patterns, or patterned along the edge of the flounce only. Warp-printed silks often appeared in them. The edges of the silk flounces were usually pinked in scallops (Plate 3). Although light and delicate shades of silk still continued to be used all through the 1850s and early 1860s, there was a general increase in richness and depth of colour, although the combination of more than two colours in the woven designs was not usual. The combination of

1.   Evening dress, blue and white striped silk, 1841–3

The pointed waistline, the short tight sleeve set low on the arm, the low neckline, trimmed with flat folds of material which repeat the pointed line of the waist are marks of the style of the early 1840s, although the trimming at the neck, usually called à la Sevigné was a detail continuing from the 1830s. The headdress is a narrow scarf of Honiton appliqué lace and roses. The shawl on the chair is cream twilled silk with sewn-on narrow borders woven in colours.

2.   'Portrait of a Gentleman', by William Huggins, 1842.

The frock coat, a darker colour than the trousers, has a velvet collar and the fitting sleeve, here with a slit cuff, of the 1840s and early 1850s. The waistcoat of figured silk has a background pattern of zig-zag lines like that in Plate 42. This portrait shows a scarf cravat fastened with a pin. The tip of the chin-high collar of the shirt is just visible.

(By courtesy of the Walker Art Gallery, Liverpool)

black with a single dark, rich colour is often found in silks of the 1850s. Floral patterns are often figured against a checkered ground. A fabric of great richness which was fashionable in the

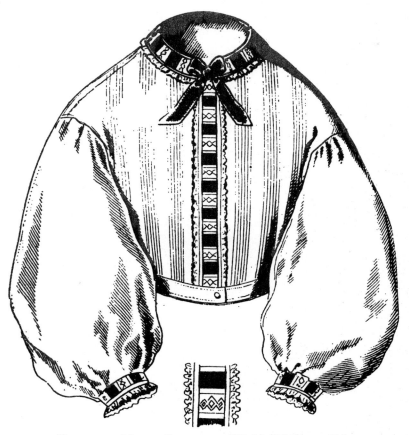

FIGURE 4.—MUSLIN CHEMISETTE (*World of Fashion, 1863*)
Neck, front, and sleeves trimmed with insertion through which a cerise velvet ribbon is drawn.

1850s was velvet-figured silk (Plate 16a). The silk, usually a dark silk—purple, brown or green—was figured in cut and uncut velvet in black, giving a fabric of great richness. The heavier, plainer silks, corded or watered, were much used in the early 1860s. Silks, warp-printed with a single flower design, in deeper shades of the ground colour were also much used in the 1860s and silks with small woven sprig patterns, checks and stripes. For evening wear, lighter silks, silk muslin, gauze and crêpe were also used. (Up to the 1860s the two forms crape and crêpe both appear for fabrics, usually transparent silk, which have a crinkled surface. From this time crape began to refer to the black and white mourning fabrics only and all other fabrics of this kind were referred to as crêpe. To avoid confusion the spelling crêpe is used throughout this book.)

FIGURE 5.—GARIBALDI BODICE (*Queen, 1864*)
White muslin braided with black or colour.

Printed muslins were amongst the many materials used for dresses with flounces *à disposition* and were rather more fashionable than in the 1840s. The printed patterns were usually light floral sprays closely printed on the ground, but the flounces were more heavily patterned. There was a strong influence of the fashionable cone design of the shawl in many of the printed muslins of the 1850s (Plate 4). Like the muslins of the 1830s, the printed patterns were often on checkered muslin. The patterns of this decade were often limited to a single colour, in many different shades. White muslin, plain or embroidered, continued in use for evening and dinner wear, and net and lace were also worn for evening dress. Machine-made lace and machine-embroidered net and muslin were all used in increasing quantities. Heavier cotton materials, white piqué and nankeen, were used for informal summer dress in the early 1860s.

Light woollen fabrics, also, were popular for summer holiday wear. Plain white alpaca was much used for dresses of this kind and is one of the characteristic fabrics of the 1860s.

By 1860 the first successful aniline dyes were colouring the fabrics of Victorian dress. The early colours, magenta and solferino, appeared in fabrics of the early 1860s, often in combination with black or white, and sometimes in unexpected places. "Magenta the favourite shade for coloured petticoats this winter" (*Englishwoman's Domestic Magazine*, 1860). Another colour of the 1860s was a bright blue which was often used with white. Scarlet and black, or scarlet, black and white, were also popular for the more informal wear and for outdoor wear.

The trimmings of dress in 1850 were mostly fringed trimmings. The fringes often formed a pointed shape on the front of the bodice, but with a different line from the trimmings of the 1840s. The 1850s trimmings start low on the shoulder and meet in a point above the waist, or descend to the waist, sometimes with overhanging lappets. The line, whether to the waist or not, is always a wide V-shape, in contrast to the long narrower V-shape of the 1840s. As the sleeves opened at the wrist, the opening was often shaped by flounces falling from the sleeve which was cut to fit the upper arm. The sleeve flounces were often fringed, and trimmed with bows of ribbon (Plate 3). Bows and pleated bands of ribbon were also used for general bodice trimmings. Many of the jacket bodices fastened with elaborate buttons.

The epaulettes which appeared at the shoulder from 1858 were often emphasized by trimmings of braid, cord, or bead ornament. Applied braid, usually black, or black stitching, in bold arabesques and geometric patterns was often used for trimming the hems of dresses in the early 1860s (Plate 21). Tabbed trimming was particularly used for skirts which were looped up, and for the petticoats worn beneath. Black braid on white piqué was particularly popular for both children's and adults' wear in summer. Black lace used in appliqué on white, and white lace on black, were also popular as trimming for dresses in the 1860s. The black lace was often now black silk Maltese lace. Lace of all kinds—but much of it now machine-made—appeared as trimming on evening dresses.

Jacket bodices of the 1850s which had an open neckline were worn with a chemisette beneath (Fig. 6). This had a plain round neck, and was shaped to a blunt point at the waist, back and front. When the neckline was high and closed, a small collar was worn. These accessories were of muslin, decorated with various types of embroidery, most of it less delicate than the embroidery of the 1840s. But there was also a fashion for plain linen collars in the late 1850s and early 1860s (Plate 5). Small silk cravats were worn round the neck (Plate 20) and white muslin cravats in the early 1860s. "Very pretty little cravats are worn, made of ribbon brocaded. ... A cravat is almost indispensable with the narrow sticking-up collars or with those the points of which alone are turned down in front" (*Englishwoman's Domestic Magazine*, 1864).

A great wealth of undersleeves of the 1850s and early 1860s has survived. During the 1850s, undersleeves became both longer, so that they extended from elbow to wrist, and much fuller. Their size increased with the widening sleeve; the closed, balloon-like shapes of about 1860 were about 18 inches long with a width of 18 inches gathered into the wrist-band. There are two types: those closed with a band at the wrist, and those open like the sleeves themselves. Those that have a band at the wrist and then a frill to fall over the wrist are likely to be from the early 1850s. Those ending with the band are likely to be from the late 1850s and early 1860s. The openwork embroidery, with a pattern of rather large holes overcast with stitching—usually known as *broderie anglaise*—belongs to this period and was much used for undersleeves (Fig. 7). Examples of it from the early 1850s are usually on light muslin; later a denser cambric was used for it. Cambric, muslin, lace and net were all used for undersleeves. They were a very important dress accessory of these years, and no dress with open sleeves is complete without them.

FIGURE 6.—MUSLIN CHEMISETTE (*Englishwoman's Domestic Magazine, 1854*)
Embroidered in cotton of two or three different thicknesses.

FIGURE 7.—ENGLISH EMBROIDERY (*Englishwoman's Domestic Magazine, 1853*)
Openwork embroidery in cotton on muslin, with the holes overcast and
the edge of the work in buttonhole stitch, later called *broderie anglaise*.

An important change in the workmanship of dresses came in
the 1860s. The sewing machine had been invented in the 1840s,
first with a chain stitching and then with a lock stitch. Machine
stitching rarely appears on dresses before 1855, but after 1865 it
is usual. Both chain and lock stitching appear on dresses throughout the rest of the period.

CHAPTER 3

DRESSES — 1865-75

BY 1865, the wide crinoline-supported skirt was in its last phase. It became more and more gored and, by 1865, some dresses had the front and side of the skirt set without pleats at the waist and all fullness swept to the back. The beginning of a new skirt form came in the same year. "Skirts are either made double as tunic dresses or single having the appearance of tunics, which is easily done by trimming" (*Ladies' Treasury*, 1865). In the following year trimming was still serving to break the ground of this new fashion: "There is no style of trimming more fashionable at the present moment than this simulating of tunics and upper skirts upon dresses of rich silks" (*Queen*, 1866). Change came also to the bodice. The waistline had been rising a little above its natural level during the early 1860s and by 1865 it was high enough for the fashion journals to announce that "the style of the empire" was about to return.

This higher waistline penetrates most dresses of the late 1860s. The other change which is usually apparent in dresses of the late 1860s is a changed neckline. The evening neckline changed from the deep, low curve over the shoulder to a form much more nearly square. In day dress the bodices remained high and plain, but by 1868 a square opening was beginning to appear, filled in with a high chemisette of muslin. Or a square, yoked effect was given to a high bodice by trimming in braid, fringes, ruches of ribbon and appliqué of lace. The bodices had short, round waists; an average measurement from shoulder to waist was fourteen to fifteen inches.

The fashion of wearing a white bodice and coloured skirt continued from the early 1860s. The Swiss belt appeared in a bodice form, with shoulder-straps added to a broad waistband with falling sash ends at the back. The waistband was a conspicuous part of dress in the late 1860s. Contrasting belts—like the Swiss belts—or long sashes were often worn with white muslin dresses, and continued fashionable until 1870. During the late 1860s, belts had large bows at the back, with long, wide ends falling over the skirt, or several wide tabs, like long basques. They were made either as part of the dress, matching it, or as separate accessories to be added to it. The fashion for long sash ends was so general that the trimming of skirts sometimes simulated sash ends, just as it simulated a tunic. Fichus of net and tulle which were worn over dress bodices often had long ends at the back.

The sleeve of day bodices was usually tight and plain in the jacket sleeve form, and was cut in two sections with a front and a back seam. Epaulettes remained at the shoulder for some years, but became rare after 1870. With the tight sleeves, long full undersleeves disappeared and short cuff-like sleeves took their place. These were worn beneath the dress sleeve, with their embroidered edge just visible at the wrist, which was sometimes open a few inches at the seam. Very narrow collars, round or pointed, were still worn with the high bodices. Muslin chemisettes filling the square open neckline were made to wear beneath the dress, usually with a back fastening; over the dress lace and muslin fichus were worn. The muslin used was often stiffer than that of the earlier collars and chemisettes. It was trimmed with insertions of lace. Much of the lace was now machine-made, although some bobbin laces, usually Valenciennes, Maltese or Honiton, were still used. Black velvet ribbon was much used with lace, threaded through it, lace-edged, or as a background for appliqué of white lace. Less hand-embroidery appeared in accessories of this date. Machine embroidery appeared in increasing quantity. Ready-made frillings of muslin and cambric were available from the mid-1860s. They were particularly useful and used for underwear, but they also appeared in the necks and sleeves of dresses from this time until the end of the century.

The sleeves of evening dress were short and almost disappeared altogether beneath the trimming of lace and ribbon which edged the neck and almost covered the low, short-waisted bodice.

Until 1868, this high-waisted style with the skirt fitting more closely at the waist was plain and slightly angular in its construction and trimming. The overskirts or tunic bodices hung in

3. 'The Empty Purse' by James Collinson, 1857

The dress in two shades of pale blue shows trimmed pagoda sleeves with ribbon-threaded under-sleeves and a skirt with pinked flounces à *disposition. The bonnet which leaves the front part of the head uncovered is the fashionable style sloping towards the back of the head, with trimming inside the brim. It is worn with a dark brown bonnet veil. On a stand on the stall is a newly fashionable hat. The purse of the title closely resembles the purse in Plate 33, and one of its rings is in the woman's right hand. On the stall is a parasol fan, and the ends of a pair of embroidered braces can be seen on the wall.*

(By courtesy of the Trustees of the Tate Gallery, London)

(left)   4.   Printed muslin day dress, 1853–5
The checkered muslin is printed in purple and mauve in a pattern of roses, the flounces à disposition showing them shaped into the ubiquitous cone design of the shawls. Narrow borders matching the flounces trim the bodice. The sleeves are a wide version of the pagoda form with a puff above the deep frill of the opening. The fringed silk parasol is a carriage parasol with a folding handle.

(below)   5.   'Travelling Companions,' by Augustus Egg. c. 1860
The two dresses, each worn over a large crinoline, appear to have matching, three-quarter length coats with large open sleeves, trimmed down the outer seam. The very narrow plain collars, fashionable in the late 1850s and 1860s are worn with narrow neck ribbons. The small round hats with single feathers would be regarded as particularly suitable for young women at this time.
(By courtesy of the Museum and Art Gallery, Birmingham)

6. 'The Ball on Shipboard,' by J. J. Tissot, exhibited 1874
This painting shows how many different styles could be worn at a single moment for a single occasion. The two women standing in the foreground show the overskirt draped in an apron front and looped in puffs over a bustle. They and the figure standing on the left have long fitted sleeves; most of the other dresses have the elbow-length sleeve with elaborate frillings. The new cuirass bodice appears on the woman coming up from the lower deck and on the standing figure on the left though hers may be a jacket over a dress, not a bodice. There are plain, narrow-brimmed sailor hats resembling those worn by some of the men, worn tilted up at the back, but most of the hats or bonnets, are worn at the new angle, perched high with a backward tilt. A parasol with a knobbed ferrule lies on a chair. The men wear either the straw sailor hat or the informal bowler hat with highly curved brim.
(By courtesy of the Trustees of the Tate Gallery, London)

pointed forms. Some of the dresses of this period were of princess form, that is a dress with bodice and skirt cut in one without a waist seam. They fastened with a central or diagonal fastening from neck to hem. The looped-up skirt of the early and middle 1860s was no longer worn. Instead, a shorter form of dress was made as a walking dress, which usually had the double skirt. This was almost a necessity, because the fashionable dress was so constructed, with front and sides gored and full widths pleated at the back, that the skirt was thrown back into a train. The

FIGURE 8.—BUSTLE, CRINOLINE AND PETTICOAT (*Queen, 1869*)
(*Left*) Crinoline of figured cotton and watchspring steels, adjustable by front lacing; (*Centre*) Bustle of linsey with steels; (*Right*) Horsehair petticoat with flounced back breadth forming bustle, for wearing under short costume.

trained skirts for afternoon dresses were often single skirts. The evening dress skirts were usually double, or else had a tunic bodice. Muslin or some other light and open fabric was often used over silk for the overskirt or tunic. By 1868, deep flounces at the bottom of the skirts were becoming fashionable.

By 1869, this transitional style of the late 1860s had passed. The half-crinoline that was still worn beneath the skirt diminished still further to a bustle during 1868 (Fig. 8). The steel framework which had replaced the earlier horsehair petticoats was being gradually replaced by horsehair bustles and petticoats, now usually referred to in the fashion journals by their French names, *tournures* or *jupons*. "The reign of Crinoline may be said to be now completely at an end; the skeleton skirt is a thing of the past; a small jupon of puffed horsehair or merino with a few steels at the bottom is all that is required" (*World of Fashion*, March 1868). Between 1865 and 1875, the supporting structures of the skirt were much less uniform in shaping and extent than the earlier framework of the crinoline. A dress which still survives with its own supporting bustle should never be separated from it, for this particular bustle was, and still is, essential for the shaping of the skirt.

During the years 1868 and 1869, the bustle and the material of the overskirt gave a new line to the skirt and set the form of the dress for the early 1870s. The overskirt was looped up over the bustle at the back and the effect was to shape the skirt into curved billowing lines (Plate 6). The underskirt, generally narrower than the skirt of the mid-1860s, was gored and sewn to the waistband plain at front and sides. The overskirt, shorter than the underskirt, was still either a separate skirt from the waist or attached to the bodice of the dress. It was looped up each side so that it fell in front as a draped apron, and bunched over the bustle at the back. By 1870, "All dresses for morning, noon and night have the inevitable panier, or tunic panier that is a tunic which can be drawn into a panier, which reaches to the apron, simulated or otherwise in front. . . . From satins to serges all have tunics, looped up temporarily or drawn up, and the apron" (*Ladies' Treasury*, 1870). This bunched and billowing effect was increased by the full basques of the bodice or by a belt with basques, which resembled a very short overskirt. In addition, the centre back of belt or bodice was often trimmed with a large bow. Evening dresses often had two or three overskirts.

The double-skirt form continued for the first years of the 1870s in a variety of forms. It might be a separate overskirt; or joined with the underskirt to the waistband; or it might be the extension of the bodice in a tunic, the form usually called a polonaise. The overskirt—whichever of these forms it took—could be open at the front, curving over the underskirt, or closed. It was usually looped up at the sides to form a draped apron front (Plate 6).

By 1873, there was again the mark of change in the skirt. "Polonaises are still popular and where not worn the back breadths of the dress have a deep pouf and the flounces at the back reach this pouf. This is managed by cutting the two back breadths of the dress a yard longer than the others. They are joined in the centre and pleated to the sides and looped with tapes underneath" (*Ladies' Treasury*, 1873). This pleating up of the longer back breadths of the dress by tapes from the waist to the lower edge of the pouf is a construction of the mid-1870s. From 1874 there was a tying back of the front of the skirt by pairs of tapes, which continued to the end of the decade and beyond. During the next year this tying back of the skirt was developed to draw the dress more tightly round the body in front, while the puffing at the back diminished, fullness being brought together in pleats at the back to fall into a narrow train.

Trimmings were used with great lavishness in the dress of the 1870s, and gave it much of its form and character. Dresses which had a single skirt simulated the lines of an overskirt in the trimming. From 1873, the trimming divided the skirt into two halves. The trimmings on the front were arranged apron-wise, usually a series of flounces forming curved or straight lines across the front section, with a different series of flounces or puffings at the back, and the division often marked by another band of still different trimming. The front might be plain with applied bands of trimming only and the back a series of flounces. Some dresses of the mid-1870s had the addition of a wide scarf, "a tunic scarf", which was attached to the waist and tied beneath the puffing at the back or looped up the back of the overskirt.

The short-waisted bodice became less worn for day dress after 1870. The sash with large bows and long ends was passing out of use by 1870, and the basqued belts were disappearing two or three years later. A jacket bodice with its own basques falling over skirt and overskirt was generally worn. The bodice became more varied in form. "The plain high bodice was long the only one made for all but dressy evening toilets, when it was replaced by a low one; now this is no longer so and dress bodices are made of so many different shapes that it is difficult to decide which is in fact the most fashionable. . . . Some are open in the shape of a heart, some are square, some with revers, like coats. . . . There are jacket bodices, bodices with points, tunic bodices made without any waist and in the princess shape. . . . Jacket bodices are cut in a number of various shaped basques and lappets" (*English-woman's Domestic Magazine*, 1870). The bodice lengthened, and by 1874 the front was extending well below the waist and was shaped to fit the figure more closely. This was known as the cuirass bodice. Together with the tightening lines of the tied-back skirt, it gave a new form to dress by 1875. The cuirass effect was heightened by having the sleeves of a different material. The very short-waisted bodice continued to be worn for evening dress, although this, too, sometimes showed a basqued form until the waistline lengthened in 1874.

The necklines of day dresses showed much variety between 1870 and 1875. They were generally open and cut square; but some were cut in a deep V-shape, often with revers. The opening was filled with a chemisette of muslin, net or lace. Some of the higher bodices with revers or a V-shaped opening had only a wide pleated frill at the neck opening. Evening dresses which were not for full evening or ball dress often had the low, square neckline at the front, but were cut high at the back like the neckline of day dresses. In the evening dresses this was left open, but outlined with pleated frillings of net or lace. For ball dress the neckline continued to be low and square, with the sleeve often no more than a band crossing the shoulders beneath the trimmings of the neckline. From 1869, a sleeve open at the wrist, and a pagoda form of sleeve with full open flounces falling from the elbow, appeared on both day and evening dress. With these open sleeves, full open undersleeves of lace or net were worn. In day dress the close jacket style of sleeve continued to be worn often with an ornamental cuff.

The bodices of day and evening dresses were lined, usually with white cotton; but silk was used for the lining of the more expensive dresses and particularly of evening dresses. The fastenings of bodices of day dresses continued to be at the front. When bodice and skirt were joined, the skirt usually fastened in front on the left; after 1870, when a jacket bodice with a separate skirt was the more usual form, the skirt fastened at the back. Evening bodices were still mostly fastened at the back, but during this period many of them were fastened in front like the day dresses. Front-fastening bodices were usually boned with two short bones on each side of the opening, a bone at each side seam, and sometimes bones at the front edges. Back-fastening bodices were boned at the centre front with one or two bones at each side. Less or more bones were used according to the type and quality of the dress, but the boning generally was light and short. The back of the bodice was usually cut in three sections, but cutting with a centre back seam in four sections began to appear in some bodices by 1870. By 1874, the darts shaping the bodice began to extend below the waist, and horizontal darts at the sides appeared. After 1870, bodices, which were not jacket bodices, often had basques made to tuck inside the skirt. Inside waistbands were sewn into bodices from the late 1860s onwards and the names of the dressmakers began to appear on them.

Skirts, whether separate, set on to a waistband, or joined by a waistband to the bodice, usually had a width at the front set plain, a number of gored sections at each side, shaped towards the back and pleated on to the waistband, and at the back one or two plain widths, which in lighter materials were set with gathering, not pleating, at the centre back. Some skirts were lined throughout; others were lined at the hem only. The lining was often of rather stiff muslin. The hems of day dresses were still usually braided. Inside the skirts there may be two sets of tapes and loops; those which work vertically, holding the upper part of the back of the skirt in the puff formed by gathering or pleating this into the side seams, which may be found from 1872; and those which work horizontally, tying across the back breadth of the skirt, to draw the front more closely over the body, from 1874. Tapes, one or two pairs only, are found occasionally in dresses of this period before these dates, showing the beginning of this device for drawing and controlling fullness at the back of the dress.

The polonaise form, with the bodice of the dress extending to form an overskirt, resembled an eighteenth-century form of dress and revived an eighteenth-century name for it. It also showed eighteenth-century influence in the use of printed cottons for the polonaise, with a plain cambric for the underskirt. "The novelty of the day is the revival of figured chintz worn in the top skirt of morning and costume dresses. The underskirt should match in colour the prevailing colour in the figured chintz" (*Englishwoman's Domestic Magazine*, 1871). In the winter, printed flannel was used instead of printed cotton. These dresses were called Dolly Vardens. They were used only for informal wear and were a homely rather than an elegant fashion. Coloured and striped cottons were also used for informal summer wear. Woollen materials, mostly light twilled fabrics, were used for everyday winter dress. For more fashionable day dress, silks, particularly the corded silks, were constantly worn. Poplin, a corded fabric of silk warp and worsted weft, was also a fashionable and characteristic material of the 1870s. Satin was once more fashionable for evening dress and, by 1875, there was an increasing use of velvet. In ball dresses a good deal of light muslin, gauze and net was used for the draped overskirts and flounces over a foundation underskirt of silk (Plate 7).

The silks were sometimes figured with small neat patterns in the late 1860s and there was a good deal of striped and flecked patterning (Plate 17). After 1870 plain silks were more general. The use of two shades of the same colour in a dress was a characteristic fashion of the early 1870s. Contrasting shades of the same material are also found. The colouring was nearly always pale during this period, in shades of brown, grey, mauve or blue. Between 1865 and 1867, dresses remained comparatively plain, as they had been in the early 1860s. After 1868, trimming became more conspicuous and, in the more elaborate dresses, it was used lavishly. This trimming is very characteristic of its period and bears certain strong and definite marks of date. In the late 1860s, the bodice trimming was usually on the epaulettes and in the form of a square, circular or V-shaped yoke on the plain bodice. It was in fringe, braid or lace. Lace was added in flat bands, edging a velvet ribbon or mixed with a ruching of the material of the dress. The mixing of beads with braid in appliqué or in hanging tassels was fashionable. Velvet in bands, particularly black velvet on bright colour or a deeper shade of velvet on a light colour, was much used as a trimming for the skirt. Trimming was often applied in medallion form with a combination of buttons, beads and braid. Beaded buttons are often found on dresses of this date.

From 1868, flounces began to appear on all dresses. The flounces were themselves complicated and varied in construction. They were often very deep, about nine inches below the heading and three inches above. Some flounces were gathered and applied in large ruches; but most often they were pleated, and in this form they were a constant and characteristic ornament of dresses between 1868 and 1875 (Plate 7). The pleating was arranged in many ways and combined with other ornament. It continued, although on a smaller scale for a narrower skirt, to ornament dresses of the late 1870s.

Bands of the material of the dress, with a wide piping of satin of the same shade and an edging of lace, black or white, applied flat or in pleats, were also favourite trimmings of the early 1870s. Trimmings of silk fringe were also still much used. Bows, plain or piped and lace-trimmed, were often added at every possible point of the dress, on the sleeves, at the centre of the bodice opening, and at the ends of flounces. Evening dresses were trimmed with sprays of flowers in addition to their flounces of muslin, net or lace, their ruchings and bows of ribbon (Plate 7).

CHAPTER 4

DRESSES — 1875-90

THE dress of 1875 shows a complete change in line and character from the dress of the years before 1874. The governing factor of this change was the cuirass bodice which appeared in 1874. This was a bodice which had lengthened, descending in a point back and front and lying closely over the hips instead of ending in the full basques of the early 1870s (Plate 8). This long-waisted bodice smoothed away all fullness of the dress over the hips and appeared to push the fullness of the skirt down from the upper half of the back to the lower half. The bustle, which had given shape to the skirt of the early 1870s, grew smaller and was brought lower down the skirt so that "the tournure is now arranged low down, nearly to the heels" (*Ladies' Treasury*, 1876). The back fullness flowed out in a train.

For once a fashionable term is exactly descriptive of its subject. The cuirass quality of the bodice was emphasized between 1875 and 1877 in a version which was sleeveless, or appeared to be sleeveless by having the sleeves of a different material. In evening dress, between 1877 and 1882, it was often cut to a very low point at the back and front, but curved high over the hips at the sides. As well as the cuirass shaping, there was, between 1879 and 1883, a long coat-like bodice form which fitted the figure closely, ending in a straight line below the hips. A loose-belted bodice which appeared in informal wear was an, occasional, alternative to these dominant corset-like forms.

With this new long-waisted bodice, the skirt also was tightened over the hips, so that it fitted without fullness at the front and sides. It was tied back inside, beneath the back fullness, which drew it tightly over the figure in front. The skirt was narrower and set without fullness at the waist. All remaining fullness was brought to the back to flow into a train: "that the bodice be as long-waisted and tight-fitting as possible, the skirt as scant and the train as full

7.   Evening dress, silk and muslin, 1871–2

The skirt is of pink silk and there are two overskirts of muslin, a full length skirt and an upper skirt—short at the front and longer at the back—ending with four pleated frills. This is supported by a bustle like that shown in figure 13.

8. Contemporary photograph, day dress, 1875–7
The dress is made from two materials, probably a silk and velvet, arranged in the bodice to emphasise the cuirass effect. This bodice, long and fitting over the hips is the characteristic style of the mid 1870s. The front of the skirt has the draped apron trimmed with fringe and bows.

9.   Day dress, satin and corded silk, 1882–3

This dress also shows use of two materials in slightly different shades of fawn-grey. The bodice is separate from the skirt. The construction of the two parts is shown in Plates 13 and 14. The front of the skirt is closely ruched bands of satin alternating with loose puffing and the back is formed of loose puffs above a detachable train of pleated frills. Over the hips are the draped folds in silk, the pannier draperies characteristic of the early 1880s.

10. Contemporary photograph, outdoor dress, 1886–8

The plain tailor-made dress of wool with a closely fitting bodice has the high standing collar of the last two decades of the century, the puffed plastron of the late 1880s and the pleated draping of the skirt then fashionable for the plainer dresses. The hat, one of the sailor shapes popular at this time, shows the use of coarse straw in fashionable hats. The three-buttoned kid gloves just meet the long fitting sleeve. The parasol shows the lace awning characteristic of the 1880s.

as may be" (*Englishwoman's Domestic Magazine*, 1875). The skirts of most dresses were now so long at the back that they had to be lifted up for walking. The sheath-like form of the front of the skirt was partly concealed by drapery which formed the main ornament of the dress. The usual form of this between 1875 and 1879 was a tunic or apron draped over the front of the skirt (Plate 8). Sometimes a wide sash was used in the same way. A critical contemporary comment gives more vividly than any more detailed description the aspect of this first phase of dress between 1875 and 1890: "Sashes tied at the back exactly as a woman would tie on an apron to wash dishes . . . who has not seen a gardener at work with black tight-fitting jacket and white or grey sleeves. Behold the cuirass with sleeves of a different colour. Next comes the tablier or apron and sash, exactly in form as those of a dish washer" (*Ladies' Treasury*, 1875).

The cuirass bodice was worn with a separate skirt. The polonaise of the early 1870s, a bodice with a skirt attached, took the new sheath-like line and was worn as well as the separate bodice and skirt form. Some of the polonaises of the late 1870s are almost as long as the dress itself and are then almost indistinguishable from a princess dress, a form which also appeared in dresses of 1878 to 1880, particularly in informal indoor styles, which were forerunners of the teagown. These three forms of dress may all be found in dress between 1875 and 1890, but the construction of dresses at this time is confusing, and dresses will be found which have a princess form for the back, but a separate bodice in front; or sometimes they may have a princess front and a bodice detached from the skirt at the back. As in the early 1870s, the tunic drapery of the skirt could be attached to the bodice, making it a polonaise, or it could be attached to the skirt. An overskirt completely separate from the skirt, often found in dresses of the early 1870s, is rarely found in the later, more elaborately draped, forms.

The different phases within this period are marked by the changes in the fullness, construction and drapery of the skirt. Complete change came only in the late 1880s, when the skirt at last shed its looped and swathed tunics above and its supporting structures beneath. The movement towards this change is, however, apparent throughout the 1880s. The dresses which are significant, which prepare the way for the newer, freer style, are the simpler dresses, the informal cottons and light woollens worn for seaside and country holidays, the tailor-made dresses of woollen cloth (Plate 10). "All dresses—be they of habit cloth, tweed, serge or any woollen material—are however made in a simple and in many cases almost severe style; perfect fit and excellence of workmanship alone being relied on to produce the—we must say it—mannish effect, which is unhappily the prevailing taste" (*Queen*, 1883). Many surviving dresses of the 1880s show this new emphasis in their plain, untrimmed lines and excellent tailoring, and the dress of the second half of the 1880s shows its penetration into all forms of dress, which finally brought the new style of the 1890s. "All elaborate frillings and puffings are fast disappearing in favour of straight, falling lines. The under-skirt is now often completely hidden except at some point where the square apron or tunic is raised on one side" (*Ladies' World*, 1886).

For the more fashionable and formal dresses in the first phase, from 1875 to 1883, "The great aim is to make the figure as flat and sheath-like as possible and upon the block to wind as close as may be all kinds of draperies" (*Ladies' Treasury*, 1875). Between 1875 and 1879, no fullness appeared in the skirt at the sides and over the hips. In 1876 it was "at most three yards round the hem" and much of this was in the train which flowed out from the confined fullness at the back. It grew narrower and more sheath-like until 1879. The trained form appeared in all fashionable dresses during these years. "Dresses are worn trained, but they are easily looped up with hooks and loops" (*Ladies' Treasury*, 1876). From 1878 short dresses without trains began to appear, first of all for walking dress; and by 1880 the train, except in evening dress, had almost disappeared. The loss of the train gave a new line to the skirt and its draperies. Lacking the pull to the back, the skirt was no longer strained closely to the figure at the front, but fell as a straight, narrow tube, a tube concealed beneath flounces and frills and puffed and gathered bands, which were arranged in horizontal bands or in a series of deep short curves, above vertical pleating at the hem (Plate 9).

Amongst the many draped tunic forms, one style became particularly fashionable for everyday dress at this time, and remained in fashion for two or three years. This was the "handkerchief" dress, in which the tunic fell in points over a narrow kilted or pleated skirt. "At the seaside nearly all the dresses for morning wear are handkerchief ones which have been more popular than ever this summer. They are made in all materials, washing ones chiefly" (*Sylvia's Home Journal*, 1880). The dresses were made in material which was made in squares for this purpose. Another style, which became a general form, was a tunic looped up in two puffs or panniers over the hips. This was a style which marked the beginning of the second phase of this period, the movement away from the sheath-like skirt. The panniers may be part of a polonaise or they may be attached to the skirt (Plate 9). They brought to dress a widening of the hip line, a concentration of fullness at the hips, which once more needed the support of a bustle. Pannier draperies were a revival, with a difference, of the polonaise of the early 1870s. They were also a conscious revival once again, of a style of eighteenth-century dress, an influence which is recurrent in the fashionable dress of the 1880s. "Very effective on the green grass are the Pompadour cottons over plain coloured petticoats. They are simply made. The skirts are flounced and sometimes edged with lace, the tunic sometimes a Watteau, merely looped up at the sides and back, opening up at the front" (*Queen*, 1880).

The complex construction of draperies over the skirt had, by 1885, already become less trimmed, though more voluminous. The panniers of the early 1880s were sometimes constructed with a puff at the back but often ended at the back in "waterfall" draperies, that is, with the back breadth of the skirt pleated closely at the top into a narrow section at the back of the waist, the pleats being held together by tapes at the back of the dress. Pleated trimmings which had persisted throughout the period from the early 1870s, now became pleated skirts or overskirts. "Kilted or box-pleated skirts with vest bodice are the most usual, the long, pointed and very gracefully-draped shawl-shaped tunics being decidedly the favourite" (*Sylvia's Home Journal*, 1885). This shawl-shaped drapery resembled the drapery of the handkerchief dresses of the early 1880s, but was fuller and on a larger scale.

The apron-draped front appeared again on the new skirt of the mid-1880s, as it had also on the skirts of the mid-1870s, and on the skirts at their narrowest about 1880. In the late 1880s there was a fashion for asymmetrical drapery: "Skirts now never have two sides alike" (*Lady's World*, 1887).

The shaping of the skirt was given by a bustle. It began to appear in 1880, increased in size to 1887—when it began to diminish—and disappeared with the new shaping of the skirt in 1889. "Our best dressed women . . . eschew drapery, even sashes, but accept the plain falling skirts, just as they are, with no dress improver and often with no steel; though a short thin one, eleven

FIGURE 9.—BUSTLES AND PETTICOATS (*Myra's Journal, 1884*)
(*Left to Right*) Petticoat of grey alpaca with crossed steels; tournure of stiff muslin; tournure of red material in flounces with section each side for buttoning on to petticoat; evening petticoat of cambric.

inches from the waist and measuring twelve inches long is an improvement" (*Woman's World*, 1889). Unlike the bustle of the early 1870s, which spread across the width of the back in a wide shallow curve, the 1880s bustle was a narrower structure, which hung down the centre of the back, or was part of the construction of the dress itself, hooped steels often being inserted in the skirt lining to give the fashionable line (Fig. 9). Bustles were also made of horsehair and of wire.

The construction of skirts throughout the period was complicated and various. In 1875 the skirt was shaped in gores so that there was no fullness at the waist at front and sides; the back, usually two widths, was set in a deep box pleat, a construction which continued until about 1880. These skirts were often unlined except at the hem, where a stiffened "demi-petticoat" was added to give the flow of the train. A "balayeuse" or pleated frill of muslin, white or matching the dress, was also added to protect the hem. During this period of trained dresses, from 1876 to 1882, the train was often made detachable (Plate 14). An outside pocket was sometimes added low down the skirt at the back in dresses of 1876 to 1878. For the rest of the period, it would perhaps be true to say that generally there is no real skirt at all, but an application of drapery and trimming to a lining or foundation. It was this foundation, usually stiff muslin, cotton satin, alpaca or silk, which gave the functional width of the skirt, the limit of distance which one leg made in front of the other. Nearly all the skirts of the late 1870s have pairs of tapes inside across the back breadths for their tying back. These tapes continued to be used throughout the 1880s, to keep the fullness of the skirt in place over the bustle.

The skirts of this period are formed by their draperies, which show great variety, ingenuity and elaboration. Certain types of trimming are, however, characteristic of the different phases. Narrow and closely pleated flounces are found as part of the ornament on the majority of dresses between 1875 and 1885. Between 1875 and 1880 they were usually combined with flatly draped folds of material, falling in curves. By 1880, silk fringe was less used, but chenille fringe was fashionable between 1880 and 1885. Lace reappeared, gathered in soft frills and flounces, and was used in large quantities on dress throughout the early 1880s. The flat folds of material were succeeded by flounces, gathered at top and bottom, forming puffed bands over the skirt. These were often combined with the pleated flounces (Plate 9). This type of trimming may be found from 1875, but it was chiefly used between 1879 and 1883. After 1884, the skirt draperies became looser and freer. Instead of layers of narrow pleated flounces the whole skirt fell in pleats, and the tunic, still draped over it, fell in plain folds. Lace still edged the draperies in some dresses, but the period of lavish trimming for day dresses was over by 1885. Loops and bows of ribbon may be found everywhere on dresses of the early 1880s.

Up to 1885, evening dresses could hardly show more trimming than day dresses, and differed only in décolletage and fabric. In the late 1880s, the style for many of the evening dresses, particularly those made of the heavier fabrics, was a long tunic open at the front to reveal the front panel of the skirt. This was often very richly ornamented, particularly in the elaborate bead embroidery fashionable at this time.

The bodices of day dresses of all forms, whether cuirass bodice, polonaise or princess robe, were becoming high to the throat by 1875 (Plate 8); or, if they opened in a V-shape or revers, they were filled with a high-necked or higher V-shaped waistcoat or chemisette, of white muslin, with a high pleated or frilled collar. A high, close neckline would have a pleated white frill. By 1879 a double collar of pleated lace worn outside the dress, with one frill lying across the shoulders and the other a standing frill round the neck, became fashionable and was worn for the next few years—"throatlets of satin, edged on both sides with lace" (*Queen*, 1880). From the 1880s a large proportion of day dresses had a standing collar of the material of the dress, which grew higher between 1885 and 1890 (Plate 10). This was finished by a narrow white frilling sewn inside on plainer dresses. Small capes and yoke-like collars of lace were worn in the early 1880s and also gathered frills of lace at the neck. Jabots of lace falling down the centre front of the bodice were fashionable in the mid-1880s, and lace cravats tied with a bow in front. A neckline cut low and square in front, but high at the back, continued to be fashionable for evening dresses in the late 1870s; but this was less worn by the mid-1880s and, in 1887, a writer in the *Woman's World* was remarking that "square and heart-shaped bodice openings in front are going out of date and the choice lies between a smart tea-gown and full dress". Ball dresses were low at the back and at the front; they were cut round or slightly square in the late 1870s and early 1880s, but by the mid-1880s they often had a deep V-shaped line or a heart-shaped curve in front. Sleeves were almost non-existent in full evening dress for most of the period, but they were beginning to reappear by 1890.

Sleeves of day dresses were generally long and fitting, with a trimmed cuff, which became less conspicuous by 1880; narrow sleeves with plain cuffs were general for most of the 1880s (Plate 10). These were long to the wrist until 1883, and then were often shorter, ending between the wrist and the elbow. By 1889, sleeves were beginning to rise above the shoulder in a small puff, a detail characteristic of the early 1890s until 1893 (Plate 11). Sleeves ending at the elbow with a frilled trimming, and slashed sleeves showing a different colour beneath, were worn in the late 1870s. Day bodices generally fastened at the front throughout the period, but, in 1880, "The most stylish bodices are those fastened at the back, having long basques and sleeves with puffs at the shoulders, while the fronts have a V of very closely gathered silk let into them" (*Queen*, 1880). This decorative shaping over the front of the dress was followed by the wearing of waistcoat fronts, which persisted for several years from 1883, when it was noted that: "A striking feature of the fashions of today is the introduction of the waistcoat into all costumes for morning and street wear" (*Queen*, 1883). This waistcoat front appeared in bodices for most of the 1880s: "Waistcoats . . . their outline still meets us at every turn" (*Lady's World*, 1887). Sometimes the front was like a man's waistcoat, but very often it was a plastron, either pleated vertically or gathered top and bottom, so that it made a puffed panel down the centre of the bodice, and it was either revealed by the bodice opening, or applied as a drapery over it (Plate 10). The waistcoat or plastron was in a different material in the same colour as the bodice, in a different colour of the same material, or different in both colour and fabric. Lace was also much used in this position in the mid-1880s. This type of trimming was sometimes applied to evening bodices, which in the late 1880s sometimes had a front fastening as well as a back fastening. "The stomacher style of trimming gives an easy pretext for hiding the front fastening and allowing the lacing at the back only to be visible" (*Lady's World*, 1887). By the end of the 1880s, the bodice was becoming the more important part of the dress: "It matters little how plain the skirt is; the bodice is all-important; and for dressy occasions full vests and jabots are almost a necessity" (*Woman's World*, 1889).

The bodice, whether it ended at the waist or extended into a polonaise or princess robe, was cut to fit the figure closely in narrow sections, elaborately boned (Plate 13). Bodices were almost always lined; the lining was often cotton satin, and sometimes it was striped or figured, but silk was used in some of the more expensive dresses. The back of the bodice, which had usually been cut in four sections in 1875, was, by 1880, cut in six or eight narrow sections, usually with a bone at each seam, a bone at the side seam beneath the arm and two bones each side of the front opening where the front sections were shaped by darts. Boning was sometimes inserted at the front fastening. Many of the separate bodices which ended at the waist have in the 1880s a narrow basque at the back, a continuation of the two central sections. The shoulder seams were placed far back on the shoulders.

The tight sheath-like form of both day and evening dress accounted in part for the appearance of a special form of dress in the late 1870s. This was the tea-gown. At first it was only a little more elaborate than the morning robes, but during the late 1870s it became less and less like a dressing-gown and more and more like a fashionable dress. The basic difference was that the tea-gown had a loose, unboned bodice. Many of them were in the princess form; and a "Watteau" back, falling in a wide box pleat from the shoulder (Plate 11), often appeared in these gowns in the 1880s. The growing severity of the tailor-made dresses in the 1880s also gave the tea-gown a special place as the most elaborate garment of daytime wear, as well as the most relaxed and easy of any style of dress. Tea-gowns were much worn in the 1880s and have survived in some numbers. They grew increasingly elaborate throughout the decade, as dress generally grew plainer; "Easy, soft, flowing tea-gowns" could be worn for informal dinner dress, but "It is not considered that they are in good style if they in any way suggest a dressing-gown or wrapper" (*Woman's World*, 1888). Tea jackets worn over any skirt were an alternative of the late 1880s. These also were never so loose as a dressing-jacket, but had greater ease than the usual dress bodice.

All through the period there was a fashion for using more than one material in a dress (Plate 8). Day dresses of the late 1870s might be made of two different materials of one shade of colour, for example poplin and velvet; or a check silk might be used with a satin of the same shade as the dominant colour of the check.

11. Teagown, printed muslin, 1890–2
The spotted muslin printed in mauve and green is on a foundation of white silk. The Watteau *back of the gown appeared on jackets and mantles in the 1870s, and became a fashionable detail for teagowns in the 1880s and for mantles and coats in the 1890s. The puffing up of the sleeve above the shoulder in these loose hanging sleeves is characteristic of the years 1889 to 1892.*

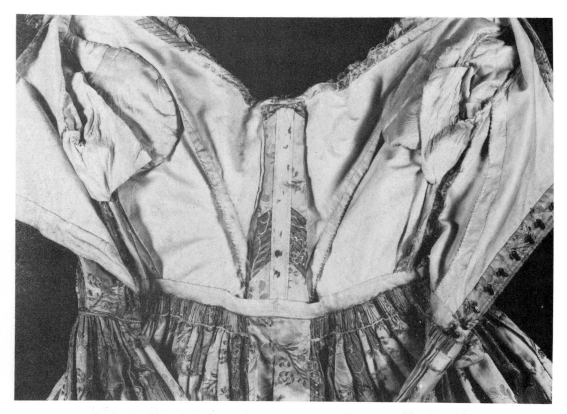

12.   Bodice construction, 1841–3

The bodice is cut in six sections, two each side of the central front seam; it is boned at the centre front and side seams only. The lining is white cotton and there are bust improvers of silk covered flannel and dress preservers of white kid. The fastening, at the back, is with hooks and eyes of flattened brass wire. The skirt lined with glazed cotton is closely pleated at the top and set on by stitching at alternate folds of the pleating.

13.   Bodice construction, 1882–3

(above right) *This shows the inside of the bodice of the dress of Plate 9. It is cut in ten sections and has twelve bones. The lining is striped cotton.*

(below right) *Detail of above showing the makers name on the waist band and the silk thread buttons.*

14. Skirt construction,
1882–3
*This shows the inside of the
skirt of the dress in Plate 9, the
lining of alpaca with stiffened
muslin at the hem and the
detachable train, and the
method of tying the skirt with
tapes across the back width.*

For evening wear, there was the combination of plain silk or velvet with figured or embroidered silk. In the late 1880s, when very rich figured materials such as velvet-figured silks were very fashionable, they were usually combined with a plain silk or satin. Only in the plain woollen tailor-made dresses were a single material and a single colour general.

Woollen fabrics had a new importance as fashionable fabrics during this period. They were used in two different ways. The sheath-like dresses of the late 1870s demanded fabrics which would fit closely and drape softly on the figure. For this the softer, lighter woollen materials were used, and these are often found, combined with silk, even in evening dresses; twilled cashmere was used chiefly in the 1870s, and the lighter woollen muslins, nun's veiling and *mousseline de laine* in the 1880s. Serge, flannel and light printed woollen fabrics were used for informal outdoor dress. The other use was of the heavier woollen fabrics, tweeds and habit cloths for the tailor-made dresses and costumes, which were the most important and significant garments in all the fashion changes of the reign. "Our home manufactures we note daily in the hundreds of neat tailor-clad figures that flit along our busy streets" (*Ladies' Gazette of Fashion*, 1881). By 1889 these tailor-made gowns with their plain severe outlines had spread from their beginnings as outdoor and travelling garments. The rougher woollen fabrics remained in use for this type of wear, but wool, in the close smooth cloths, was a fashionable material for general wear. "A tailor-made gown ... is suited to almost all occasions when morning dress is permissible. Such costumes are worn in London at the smartest weddings and afternoon parties, and it would not be out of place in a long country walk across stubble fields, or for a tour abroad" (*Woman's World*, 1889).

A fabric used for stockings and gloves for many years was given a new fashionable use in 1879 and made a new fashionable garment. The jersey, a bodice without fastening, or with a back fastening, was made in wool or silk jersey or stockinette. It provided a more sheath-like garment for the upper part of the body than was achieved in any other fabric. It was worn with a serge or flannel skirt or, in summer, a linen or cotton one, and was particularly popular for tennis wear between 1879 and 1882.

The need for materials which would drape softly meant a revival of the lighter silks. Surah, a soft twilled silk, was fashionable for most of the period. Madras or Delhi muslin, "looking ... more like a transparent brocade than anything else" (*Sylvia's Home Journal*, 1880) is often found in dresses of the late 1870s and early 1880s. Many washing materials were used in summer woollens. Natural coloured canvas, often embroidered in colour, was a particularly characteristic fabric for summer dresses in the mid-1880s. Coloured cottons with white embroidery and embroidered tussore silk, a wild silk in natural colour, were also fashionable.

Amongst the heavier fabrics, plush, a cotton velvet with a deep pile, was much worn in the early 1880s. Other heavy fabrics of frequent use were brocaded silk; satin figured in cut and uncut velvet; and *matelassé*, a silk figured so that it appears to be quilted.

Small floral patterns, closely woven, were generally used for figured materials in the late 1870s and early 1880s. The patterns tended to become larger towards the end of the 1880s, although the smaller patterns were still used. The influence of the eighteenth-century patterns can also be seen in both printed and woven fabrics. Sometimes dresses of this period will be found remade from eighteenth-century silk or printed cotton. Printed silks, woollens and cottons were all fashionable during the 1880s, in stripes, spots and striped patterns.

It was generally a period of rich and varied colour, sometimes rather harsh colour and garish combinations, but there are from the 1880s an almost equal number of dresses in very light shades. "The lighter the tint, the more elegant the gown. The skirts of plain colour are worn with bodice and wide-spreading coat tails of flowered material to match" (*Queen*, 1883). Lighter colours were more general for evening than day dress. Blue and white and red or pink and white are often found in the summer washing dresses. Many shades of blue were worn, particularly in the 1880s, and rich browns, chartreuse and olive green; but red, in rich wine and jewel-like shades, was perhaps the dominant colour of the whole period. Claret, garnet, crimson and plum-colour were used as the single colour of a dress, using two materials, velvet and satin; or they were used, particularly in the late 1870s, with a contrasting neutral shade, garnet and grey, claret and cream. A combination of bright red and dark grey was also popular in the 1880s. The lace which was used in profusion to trim the draperies of the dress, and for the collars and plastrons added to them in the early 1880s, was often coffee-coloured. Some of the lighter summer dresses were trimmed with bows and loops of brightly coloured ribbon.

CHAPTER 5

DRESSES — 1890-1900

THE change of style which set the dress of the 1890s, apart from that of the 1880s, was a change of emphasis from the skirt to the bodice. The skirt which, with its complexity of drapery, had been the main feature of dress between 1875 and 1889, now became "scanty and unimportant" in the words of a journal of 1890. From 1886, skirts became less and less trimmed, their drapery fell in plainer lines, but, except in the severer tailor-made dress for country and active wear, the double form of skirt with a draped tunic or overskirt remained until 1889. In the 1890s, this form disappeared from day dresses during the first years of the new decade, and from more formal and elaborate dresses a year or two later. The skirt now fitted closely at the waist; fullness all fell from the centre back, unsupported by any bustle or steels, plain and untrimmed, in a flowing line to the ground. It was this new line of the skirt which was the important change of the 1890s, although it was the bodice which now received fashionable attention.

The bodice generally remained a rigid, corset-like form. There was no relaxation of its boning and the waist measurements of the bodices of the 1890s are as small as in any period of the century. In day dresses the standing collar of the 1880s, which had grown higher by 1890, became higher still, two inches or more, by the late 1890s, and remained high into the new century. From 1890 to 1892, the sleeves were narrow with the small puff rising above the level of the shoulder, which had already appeared in 1889. From 1892, the upper half of the sleeve began to swell and grew wider and wider until 1896. In evening dress a short but extremely full and puffed sleeve, ending at the elbow or just above, appeared on most evening dresses between 1892 and 1897. In 1897, the fullness left the sleeves in the same way as it began, with a small puff still remaining at the shoulder; but this puff, unlike the

earlier one, spread out sideways instead of rising above the
shoulder. "All fullness has vanished save at the shoulder where
pointed and square epaulettes, puffs or butterfly arrangements
maintain their wide effect which makes the waist look small"
(*Graphic*, 1897) (Plate 40).

The waistline in 1890 was low and there was an emphasis on
vertical lines throughout the dress. The revers of the jacket
bodices, which were much worn, were often long and narrow,
and the bodice trimming formed a close, deep V-shape on the
front. By 1893 the revers of this type of bodice were becoming
larger and, as the sleeves spread out widely, the revers spread
towards the shoulder. On evening dress, revers spread as epaulettes
over short full sleeves; or a deep berthe of lace spread over them.
In 1893 there was a full sleeve which sometimes fell off the top of
the arm, so that it continued the line of the bodice across the
arm; the bodice was held over the shoulder by narrow shoulder-
straps. All possible width and ornament were given to the upper
half of the bodice, to emphasize a small waist beneath. A yoked
bodice had already appeared in 1890, and yoke shapes, square,
round or V-shaped appeared on many dresses of the 1890s. The
yoke was usually a trimming only, not a construction, and it was
often frilled. The tight fitting bodice was usual, but many bodices
were made with a loose section at the centre front over a closely
fitted lining, especially towards the end of the decade. Almost all
the fullness and looseness which appeared in the bodices of the
1890s was deceptive. The full sleeves of day dress were made on
a lining which fitted the arm. The loose bolero and open jacket
forms were often not what they seemed, but an applied trimming
of a bodice on a close-fitting boned lining. By 1897 a bolero, or
bolero effect, "appears on nearly every dress, either for morning
or evening wear, and in every variety of material from velvet to
lace (*Graphic*, 1897), and this continued to the end of the century.

There was one form of bodice which in particular developed
and flourished in the 1890s. This was the blouse. A loose informal
bodice, worn with a contrasting skirt, with or without coat or
cape, had appeared as far back as the 1860s. A loose belted tunic
had been worn in the 1880s, but by 1890 a blouse was more than
the occasional garment of informal wear. It became so much worn

that in part it lost its original difference from the bodice, and many blouses of the 1890s are as rigidly boned as any of the dress bodices. "Blouses have grown so much in popular favour during the last few years that from *néglige* garments of the loosest, baggiest and most unpretentious description they have developed into the favourite bodices of the age, making an appearance on the most important occasions . . . so much caught down and pleated and pressed into shape upon a close fitting lining that their leading characteristics have almost disappeared" (*Woman's World*, 1890). The blouse was worn with a contrasting skirt. It could be worn with any skirt, and a single skirt could have its appearance renewed by the wearing of different blouses. The blouses varied from the plainest shirt-like garments to elaborate constructions and trimmings of silk and lace. The fashion persisted throughout the 1890s (Fig. 10).

The popularity of the blouse meant a change in the component parts of the tailor-made costume. The early tailor-made costumes of the 1890s were either dresses, the bodice worn with a waistcoat or having a waistcoat front, or they were dresses with matching jackets. "Tailor-made dresses of tweed, cloth, etc., are as a rule very simple in style to be suitable for travelling and walking, but like nearly all other gowns they have waistcoats which are often of bright colours" (*Sylvia's Home Journal*, 1885). It was not until the 1890s that the form of coat, skirt and blouse was established, a form which has never since been absent from the dress of Englishwomen. The wearing of this form of dress increased during the 1890s: "This we have at least the grace to encourage from year to year . . . the coat and skirt worn with shirt and blouse. This appears this season in larger variety than ever" (*Queen*, 1893).

The bodices of evening dresses usually fastened at the back but sometimes in the front. Those of the day dresses usually fastened in front, the fastening often being on the bodice lining with the bodice front overlapping. Some have a cross-over draping. They were usually boned, with five bones at the back, a bone at each side seam and two each side of the front opening, but, unlike the bodices of the 1880s, they were, by the mid-1890s, very often without a centre back seam. The high collar often had a stiff

FIGURE 10.—BLOUSE AND FAN (*Queen Almanac, 1896*)
Blouse of white muslin with tucked and frilled front and insertions of yellow
lace; fan of painted white gauze and Honiton lace.

interlining, but in the last years of the century it often appeared as folded bands of material. The belt or waistband might also show this folded form. Belts, with the wearing of blouses and skirts, the short bolero jackets, and the emphasis on a small, neat waist, became a more important accessory in the 1890s than they had been since the 1870s (Plate 40). Buckles were used ornamentally and there was a revival of the buckle forms of the eighteenth century and the use of surviving eighteenth-century buckles.

The tea-gown continued in use for the whole of the 1890s. As in the 1880s, it differed little from the most elaborate dresses, except in the looser lines of the bodice and a tendency to keep the front-fastening princess form. Many of the tea-gowns of the 1890s were in the "Empire" style, falling loosely from a high waistline, inspired by the fashions of the early nineteenth century. This style was sometimes used for evening dress.

As the sleeves spread and gave width to the bodice from 1892, the skirt widened at the hem. The fullness was still swept to the centre back, but, by 1893, five and a half yards was often given as the usual width for the skirt at the hem. For day wear the skirt still cleared the ground, until 1898. "Happily they continue short—a blessing for which we have to thank the bicycle" (*Graphic*, 1897). But from 1898 they became longer and had to be held up in walking. Trained gowns for carriage wear were already fashionable in 1897. The plain line of the skirt now began to disappear in trimming. In the lighter materials, particularly, skirts trimmed with tucks round the skirt from waist to hem, or with apron trimming continuing as a flounce at the hem, were general by 1897. "The trimmed skirt now holds the field entirely in all dresses of this light description" (*Lady's Realm*, 1898).

The shaping of the skirt of the 1890s was achieved by gored cutting and by fitting over the hips with short darts. The number of gores in the skirt varied; double-width material was used, cut on the cross in fewer sections, but the narrower materials were cut in four or five gores at each side of the front width. But the skirt of the 1890s was given its characteristic shape, until the last two or three years of the century, mainly by the cutting of the back breadths on the cross and joining them with a seam at centre back on the cross cut. This flow at the back of the skirt was

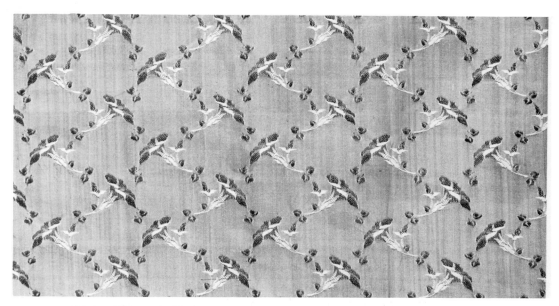

(above)   15(a).   Figured silk from dress, 1847–9
Blue and white shot silk figured in trellis pattern of convolvulus flowers.

(below)   15(b).   Printed wool from dress 1848–50 (Pl.19)
Wool printed in black, blue green and orange.

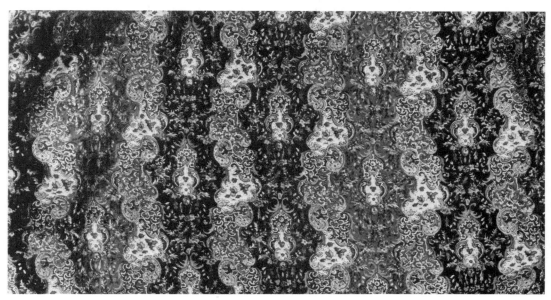

16(a). Velvet-figured silk from dress, 1853–5

Green silk figured in cut and uncut velvet in black in a cone design.

16(b) Printed muslin from dress 1853–5 (Pl.4)

Checkered muslin printed à disposition in light and dark shades of purple in a design of roses combined with the cone motif, ubiquitious in mid nineteenth-century shawls.

17. Figured silk from dress, 1862–4
Green silk, checkered in pale yellow, figured in green silk and black spotted with yellow.

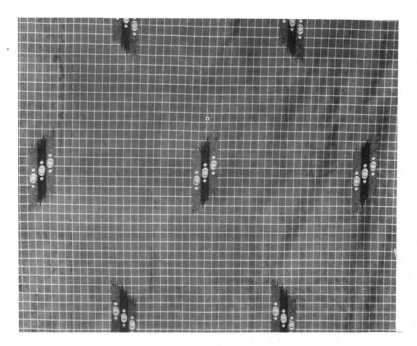

18. Figured silk from dress, 1894–6
Dull blue satin, figured in fawn and brown.

modified by the addition of secondary gores or wings in the seams in the lower part of the skirt, so that the fullness spread round the hem. This appeared as early as 1893; but it did not change the skirt line noticeably until 1897, when the fullness was lessened in the upper part of the skirt, which fitted closely over the hips, leaving the still full lower half in a flounced line at the hem. A new type of skirt which had a full circular flounce below the knee also gave the same change of line from 1897. Skirts pleated from the waist were also worn at this time, particularly for dancing. "New fan-pleated or 'sun-ray' skirts, nine yards at hem, one yard at top" were noted by the *Graphic* amongst the fashions of February 1897.

Once more the skirts were lined, often with a silk lining, and as they became fuller they were often made with stiffened interlining as well. Dress now had to please the ear as well as the eye. "One of the ambitions of dress just now is the rustle. The frou-frou of a gown is one of its desired merits" (*Queen*, 1893). The silk of the lining changed from the rustling glacé or taffeta to softer silk in 1898. "All our dresses will be mounted on the softest of linings, for to rustle we have now no desire" (*Lady's Realm*, 1898–9).

A new style was beginning to evolve in the last three years of the century. The change in line was slight but significant. The changing construction of the skirt caused it to fall in more curving lines at the hem and to fit more slimly over the hips. The bodice had lost its fullness of sleeve. In its plainer forms the dress of these years may appear as a simple style; but in fashionable wear the apparent simplicity was so overlaid with trimmings and veiled by its materials that the dress took a new character from them in reaction from the severe tailored style of the early 1890s.

There was also a change in the use of materials. Until the late 1890s, the heavier cloths—satins, richly-figured silks and stiff glacé silks—were worn, stiffly lined. In the last years of the century it was the soft, clinging materials which were chiefly used. "All clinging materials will be used and even cloth will be of a soft texture" (*Lady's Realm*, 1898–9). Velvet was fashionable and the soft, lustrous silk crêpe, crêpe-de-chine. The light open materials in silk, cotton and wool were even more characteristic. In woollen fabrics "De laine, the old mousseline—that is a thin texture of muslin, made with wool—is again seen, printed or plain" (*Ladies' Treasury*, 1894), and was a favourite material, as is seen in many surviving dresses. Muslin itself, also plain or printed, was much used. Silk gauzes and muslins were fashionable, particularly chiffon, a fine silk muslin. This material was being used for evening dress in 1890, and it became more and more fashionable, particularly for trimmings. "Everything is veiled or trimmed with chiffon, jewelled net, the flimsiest of gauzes" (*Lady's Realm*, 1898). It was used for the flimsy scarfs which were folded twice round the neck and tied in a bow or knot in front, and for frills everywhere. With these light materials a good deal of lace was also used. In the early 1890s, it appeared chiefly in deep berthes or epaulettes, or in deep flounces falling from short puffed sleeves, but in the late 1890s it was much used as part of the fabric of the dress. All types of lace were used and old lace was brought out again for another wearing on dresses and blouses of these years. "We are to use a good deal of lace, old lace and new, but the new is made to simulate the old as much as possible" (*Queen*, 1893). Lace blouses were particularly popular: "It is essential to the conduct of all good wardrobes that they possess a lace bodice, if not two, the one high, the other low" (*Gentlewoman*, 1897).

Tucks, very fine tucks round the skirt and bodice, were a particularly characteristic trimming of these years. On the tailor-made cloth dresses and coats and skirts, braiding of all kinds and appliqué of velvet were the usual trimming, and embroidery also ornamented all materials from cloth to net.

Pattern shared the general softening of outline. The warp-printed *chiné* silks were fashionable. Floral patterns in trailing lines, and floral forms loose in outline, appeared in the printed fabrics. "The plainest dresses will have floral designs trailing over them" (*Lady's Realm*, 1898). Rarely were pattern and ground of woven fabrics sharply defined; and all might be veiled by lace, net or chiffon.

Colour, too, became paler, except for the strong contrast of black and white which was fashionable for most of the 1890s. At the beginning of the 1890s, yellow had been a fashionable colour, and all shades of purple. The bright contrasts of the 1880s continued in the early 1890s, but gradually faded into paler tones. The mingling of mauve and light green, 'heliotrope and chartreuse', was particularly characteristic for most of the decade.

The change which marks the end of the Victorian period in women's dress came in the year of the Diamond Jubilee, not with the end of the century or the death of the Queen. The fashions of the last years of the century were the beginnings of a new form which did not reach its climax until the next reign and the next century.

CHAPTER 6

UNDERWEAR

THE garments worn beneath the dresses of the Victorian period are important because of their share in producing the final effect of the dress. They also show an interesting development without reference to the contemporary dress. Throughout the period there was a gradual but uninterrupted movement towards greater decoration of underwear, and a movement, slightly less certain, towards diminishing volume.

The garments may be divided into two groups: underlinen, the chemises and petticoats worn between skin and dress to protect each from the other, and at some periods to help to support the dress; and the structural underwear, the corsets, bustles and crinolines which mould or extend the human form into the shape of fashion.

Corsets were worn throughout the period and these corsets give the shape of the upper half of the dress. During the 1840s and 1850s, the corsets were long, back-lacing, with gussets over the hips and for the breasts, and with shoulder-straps. They were stiffly boned with whalebone and had a busk, long and about an inch and a half wide, in wood or whalebone, inserted at the centre front. During the 1860s, much shorter and more lightly boned corsets were worn, with the rising waistline of the dress. Front fastening was now general on a metal busk. Shoulder-straps disappeared after the 1840s. Quilted corsets were worn in this period, and scarlet, which appeared in petticoats and stockings, also penetrated to the corset. Coloured corsets were fashionable from this time onwards. Earlier examples from the 1840s and 1850s are usually in white, grey or fawn. The material was usually a strong twilled cotton or cotton satin.

By 1875, long, tightly-laced corsets were once more necessary to give the sheath-like fashionable shape, the foundation of the cuirass bodice (Fig. 11). The busk lengthened, then widened at

the base and curved outwards, giving the "spoon" busk characteristic of corsets of the 1880s and early 1890s (Fig. 12). Corsets
with back lacing only were sometimes worn because the front
fastening might show beneath the sheath-like bodice. Corsets of
1875 to 1890 were particularly strong in construction, with
elaborate cutting in sections and boning, some being reinforced
with bands of leather. They also became increasingly elegant,
made in satin or figured silk, and many of this period and in the
1890s were black, stitched in colours (Fig. 12). Trimming of lace

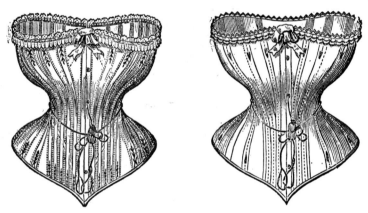

FIGURE 11.—CORSETS (*Milliner and Dressmaker, 1874*)
Izod's patent corsets steam-moulded on earthenware or metal models.

and ribbon at the top of the corset became more elaborate in the
1880s and 1890s.

In the 1890s the front busk lost the spoon-shape, becoming
narrower and straighter; but corsets were still long with complicated boning. There was also an alternative corset, shorter and
lighter, like a deep Swiss belt, sharply pointed at top and bottom,
which was worn for sport or as a *négligé* corset.

Suspenders, "English garters", were worn from the 1880s, but
were not attached to the corset until the end of the century.

Bustles were worn at the opening of the reign to support the
fullness of the skirt. These were crescent-shaped pads filled with
down or stiff frills of strong cotton satin or twill, tied round the

waist. As the skirts grew wider, support was given by increasing numbers of petticoats, stiffened by their corded weave; and, in particular during the 1840s, by a stiffened petticoat of horsehair, the crinoline petticoat. In the 1850s, hoops of whalebone were inserted into a petticoat to support the wider skirts and from this a framework, first of whalebone and later of thin flexible steels, was evolved which was now called the crinoline (Fig. 3). This framework was flattened in front in the late 1860s and became a

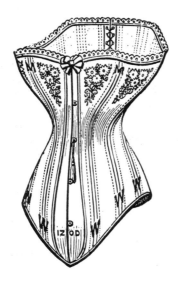

FIGURE 12.—CORSET (*Queen Almanac, 1896*)
Izod's "New Artystyque Corsets" in white or black sateen.

half-crinoline. In the 1870s, this half-crinoline swelled at the top into a bustle (Fig. 13) or a separate bustle was worn with it, and then, as the fullness left the hem of the skirt, the bustle without the half-crinoline was worn alone. The bustles of this period— the early 1870s—were usually of puffed and frilled horsehair, extending in a wide curve across the hips. During the late 1870s, no bustle was worn, but flounces were added at the base of the petticoat to throw out the hem. A bustle had returned again by 1883. The form of this was different from the bustle of ten years earlier. The bustle of the mid-1880s, "the camel's hump", was usually of steels, often mounted in a half-petticoat, which formed half-circles of short diameter, but stiff frills of horsehair were also worn (Fig. 9). Bustles disappeared about 1890, although a small pad was often inserted beneath the fullness of dresses at the centre back in the early 1890s.

Bust improvers may be found sewn inside some dresses at almost all periods, but particularly in the 1840s. Bust bodices, for wearing beneath jerseys and blouses (i.e. unboned bodices), were introduced in 1889.

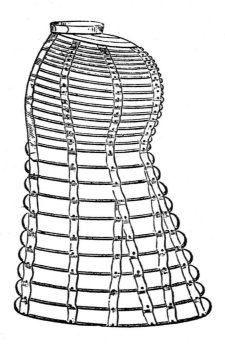

FIGURE 13.—NEW PANIER CRINOLINE (*Queen, 1870*)

Linen was still the usual material of underwear at the beginning of the period, although cotton was also used. Both materials appear in varying degrees of fineness. At this time very little ornament appeared, usually only frilling of muslin at neck and sleeves. During the middle years of the century, more cotton was used and more decoration appeared—narrow insertions and frills of openwork embroidery and, at the hems of petticoats, often a deep flounce of the large-holed openwork, *broderie anglaise*. Trimming increased during the late 1870s and 1880s, much of the embroidery now being machine-worked. Tucks were used ornamentally with insertions of embroidery and lace. Silk began to be used for underwear in the 1880s: "Underclothing is now made of soft silk and is as much trimmed with lace as our dresses, with hand embroidery most beautifully done" (*Sylvia's Home Journal*, 1880). At the same time wool also began to be used for underwear: "we wear wool not only in undergarments, where combinations fully trimmed with lace are banishing linen and cotton almost entirely, but in dresses, bonnets and cloaks" (*Woman's World*, 1888). Knitted woollen fabric was chiefly used for these woollen undergarments. By the end of the century, wool might be worn for warmth and hygiene's sake, but fashionable underwear in fine lawn, muslin and silk, trimmed with lace and embroidery and threaded with ribbons, had become still more decorated and more decorative.

Chemises were worn throughout the period. Those of the 1840s and 1850s were usually plain and voluminous and made with a square, falling flap in front, which folded down over the top of the corset. The short sleeves had a square gusset under the arm and were gathered into a band; usually were gores at the sides. After 1860, the falling flap disappeared and a round, low neckline with short front opening was usual. During the 1870s and 1880s the chemise generally became shorter, more shaped to the figure and sleeveless.

Short waist-length undergarments to cover the corset were worn mainly in the second half of the century, replacing the falling flap of the chemise. They were shaped for the waist and usually had a front opening. In the 1870s and 1880s they were called petticoat bodices, but later were known as camisoles.

Drawers were only just becoming generally worn in the 1840s. They were made with two tubular legs, the inside seams open in the upper half and the two legs linked only by the band at the waist. The legs ended well below the knees in the middle years of the century, but shortened to the knees during the 1870s. The open-legged shape continued in use until the end of the century, but during the 1880s a form with the legs seamed together, and opening at the sides to fasten together at the waist, came into use. The legs now, instead of being straight, were gathered into a band with a frill below. During the 1890s the legs were often very wide and full.

Combinations were an undergarment contemporary with the sheath-like dresses of the late 1870s. They were chemise and drawers in one garment designed to reduce the volume of underwear beneath these dresses. This was an undergarment for which knitted woollen fabric was often used. Elaborate combinations in silk and muslin with full wide legs trimmed with lace were worn in the 1890s, although in 1897 it was stated that "the fashion for wearing combinations is followed by very few people and indeed, one may say, by none of the smart set, who never really took to this form of underwear" (*Lady's Realm*, 1897).

Petticoats usually show the same shaping as the dresses they supported. At the beginning of the period some petticoats were still full-length, with a sleeveless bodice. They fastened at the back and were shaped with a pointed waistline like the dresses, with the skirt set on to the bodice in gathers or close pleating. Waist-length petticoats were, however, the more usual form for most of the period. In the late 1870s, a princess petticoat form, sheath-like in front like the dresses, was once more an alternative style, and remained in fashion until the end of the century, although the waist-length petticoat was still the general style. In the 1840s the petticoats were very full, gathered on to a shaped waistband which fastened with buttons or a drawstring at the back. An under-petticoat of horsehair was used as a support for the widening skirts; but instead of this, or as well as this, supporting petticoats of cotton, woven with a thick cording of the fabric so that they stood out stiffly to support the skirt were worn. In the middle of the century, cotton petticoats often had a hem of openwork embroidery. During the 1870s and 1880s, they usually had the tied back and flounced hems, which repeated the lines of the skirt and shared the increasing ornament of all underwear. Separate petticoat trains which buttoned on were worn in the late 1870s. Very elaborate petticoats were worn in the 1890s: "the petticoat requires as much fitting as the overskirt and, of course, like the latter, is severely tight round the top" (*Lady's*

Realm, 1898–9). At the end of the 1890s particularly, they were much trimmed with flounces at the hem.

Flannel petticoats were worn for warmth from the beginning of the reign and, from the 1860s, when scarlet flannel was popular, the flannel might be coloured. Coloured satin and alpaca were also used for petticoats, chiefly in the last quarter of the century. Quilted down petticoats were worn in winter in the 1880s.

The quantity of petticoats worn varied greatly, from the five or six used to support the skirt in the 1840s and early 1850s, when there was no crinoline frame to do most of this work, to the single petticoat which was all that could be worn beneath the dresses of the late 1870s. Sometimes even this was omitted, and flounces were attached inside the lower part of the skirt instead. With the crinoline frame, one or two petticoats were all that were needed. The number and kind of petticoats worn varied also according to dress and according to season.

19. Outdoor dress, 1848–50

The bonnet is the one shown in Plate 24. The dress shows one of the brightly printed woollen fabrics of the 1840s, a pattern of black, blue, green and orange. The mantle is green and cream shot silk, braided and fringed. The parasol of green and red shot and figured silk is a walking parasol with long handle and ferrule.

CHAPTER 7

OUTER GARMENTS

Cloaks, capes, mantles, coats, jackets, shawls and scarves

THE out-of-door garments of the Victorian woman have so much variety that for identification and dating it is perhaps easiest to divide them first according to the different main forms. First of all there were the cloaks, the true cloaks, sleeveless, all-enveloping, falling full from the shoulder, full-length or three-quarter-length; their shorter versions were the capes. There were the full-length coats, cut with sleeves and fitting the figure or the shape of the dress; their shorter versions, the jackets. Between these were garments, full-length, three-quarter-length, half-length or less, which lie somewhere between the coat or jacket and the cloak or cape, or between these and the shawl. For all these the general term mantle will be used. This tidy arrangement means to a certain extent the ignoring of contemporary fashionable nomenclature, which at one date refers to almost any outer garment, whether with sleeves or not, as a cloak, and at another refers to coats and cloaks alike as mantles.

At different periods there were different dominant forms. At the beginning of the reign the full-length fitted coat, which had been called a pelisse, had passed out of fashion, but the cloak was worn. The short cape was also worn but, during the 1840s, half-length and three-quarter length mantles of different shapes became increasingly fashionable. Jackets were worn only a little in the 1840s, appeared more often in the 1850s, but were one of the main styles of the 1860s. They were fashionable then in many forms, very short, half-length or three-quarter-length in full, loose forms, or three-quarter-length in fitted forms. At the same time, short circular capes and three-quarter-length cloaks were also fashionable. The short jacket, in new shaping with basques to fit the new lines of the dress, continued to be worn during the

1870s, and in the late 1870s extended in sheath form to a fitted three-quarter-length coat; but cloaks and capes were less worn. During the 1880s, mantles in great variety were the general form, and coats and cloaks less characteristic. These returned again in the early 1890s, and short capes were also particularly fashionable in this decade.

A cloak was often worn for comfortable out-of-door wear in cold weather in the late 1830s and early 1840s. The cloak of this date was a voluminous garment, usually falling from a yoke and not easy to distinguish from a cloak of the early 1830s. Many were of silk, lined with silk and interlined with an extra layer of wool, or padded, for warmth. To give yet more warmth, an additional cape or deep collar sometimes fell over the upper half. Other cloaks were made of woollen cloth of various weights, usually with a silk lining; only the very utilitarian ones had wool also for a lining. The seams were usually piped and there were slits for the arms. The circumference at the hem was usually between three and four and a half yards.

Some of the dresses of the late 1830s and early 1840s were made with matching capes which reached to about the level of the elbow. There were also longer capes falling below the waistline of the dress. Most of them were seamed over the shoulder and down the arm, a line and cut which made the characteristic falling curve of the 1840s, but some were shaped by darts at the neck. Silk was the usual material for them apart from those which matched their own dress. Some were lined, but a large proportion were left without lining.

The full-length cloak grew rarer during the 1840s. Three-quarter-length cloaks were worn, but cloak and cape forms were less usual than varied forms of mantle. The simplest of these mantles were very close either to the cape or the triangular shawl and had very little shaping. They were round or pointed at the back, slightly shaped for the arms and with darts or horizontal pleating at the neck. In the scarf mantle, this cape or shawl over the shoulders was extended to form scarf ends in front. Mantles of this shape, particularly in embroidered muslin, had been worn in the early 1830s. With several variations of shape and with increasing emphasis on the mantle and less on the scarf ends, they

20.   'A Walk of the Beach' by Augustus Egg, 1855–60
The round straw hat with wide turned-down brim is the hat popular for seaside wear during the 1850s. The plain loose jacket has wide open sleeves showing beneath them the full undersleeves or perhaps with this costume the sleeves of a white bodice worn with a separate skirt. A cravat is tied above the white embroidered collar. The gauntlet gloves are a style generally limited to riding and country wear.

were one of the main forms of the 1840s (Plate 19). Other mantles had cape-like sleeves, falling over a three-quarter-length cloak. They were made in silk, particularly in the changeable silk of this time, velvet or muslin. Many of the silk mantles were unlined, but the velvet ones were usually lined with silk. They were trimmed with falls of lace, with ruching, with pinked and scalloped edge, with fringes and bands of applied velvet or silk braids. The applied curving lines of fringe often suggested a series of capes. Fringed trimmings became increasingly popular by 1850. Apart from the use of black lace with coloured silks the trimmings usually toned with the material of the mantle.

These mantles bear a variety of names—*visite, paletot, pardessus*. One may work out by careful comparison of fashion engravings and fashion notes what appears to be the difference between them, only to find that, by the next year or even the next month, what was called a *visite* now appears identical with a *pardessus*, and a *paletot* is something quite different.

Coats and jackets were not a great deal worn in the 1840s. They were mostly three-quarter-length or a little shorter, usually with fitted bodice and sleeves and a skirt full over the hips. There was also a loose jacket with wide sleeves, for evening wear, which at this time was usually called a *sortie de bal*. The same term, when used twenty years later, meant a circular cape, worn with evening dress.

Jackets grew more fashionable during the 1850s when the dress also often had a jacket bodice. As the sleeves of dresses opened out into the wide pagoda forms which were fashionable in the mid-1850s, the shaping of the jacket bodice approached that of a mantle with a fitted bodice and full skirt.

A new type of jacket, falling loose and straight from the shoulder with wide sleeves, plain in line and with little trimming, short or three-quarter-length, appeared in the second half of the 1850s; and by 1860 jackets of this kind (Plates 20 and 21), and fitted jackets with close or open sleeves, were very much worn.

Coats, either long, ending a few inches above the hem of the dress or three-quarter-length, were also worn by 1860 in both forms, hanging loose from the shoulders, or with a fitted bodice and a skirt spreading over the full skirt of the dress. The sleeves

21. Outdoor Dress, 1864–6

The small round hat of velvet, trimmed with a small feather is like the hats of Plate 5. The jacket falls like that of Plate 16, loose and full from the shoulders into the line of the skirt. It is of grey woollen cloth, trimmed with black velvet and braid and has a characteristic detail of coats and cloaks of 1860s, trimming falling from the neck down the centre back. The skirt of the dress, which is of purple wool shows another detail of these years, the ornamenting of the hem in interlaced geometric pattern, carried out here in black stitching and black velvet. The woollen braid which protects the edge of the hem can also be seen.

22. Evening mantle, plush, 1885–9

This mantle made by Lewis and Allenby is of red plush lined with satin. It shows a dolman style of sleeve, which is cut as part of the back to the elbow and then shaped in a short sleeve for the lower part of the arm. There are long scarf ends in front and the back is divided so that the short central section rests on the bustle. The trimming is gold cord and beads with an edging of feather, which is often found on mantles, particularly evening mantles, of the 1880s.

23.   Cloth cape, 1894–6
This is a circular cape of dark fawn cloth, trimmed with cut-out appliqué of the same material. The high circular collar is a distinguishing feature of dress and evening capes and mantles of the second half of this decade and the first few years of the next century.

FIGURE 14.—(*Punch, 1855*)
CHARLES.—"Figure indeed! What's a fellow to do? A man must wear
something. Hats and coats are out of the question—they are really so very
effeminate."

(Reproduced by permission of *Punch*.)

were either loosely fitting sleeves with cuffs, or wide-open sleeves. Some of the coats were belted at the waist, particularly in the second half of the 1860s.

The jackets and coats, particularly some of the shorter jackets, often had a double-breasted form, with buttons and pockets more conspicuous than they had been for a long time on women's dress. "Why do ladies affect gentlemanly attire, I wonder . . . why do they not leave to the sterner sex the paletots and pocketed jackets with large buttons, which are their special attributes.

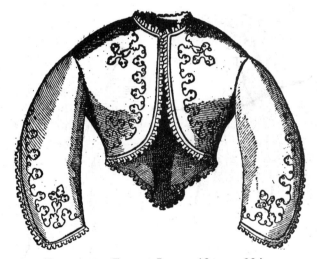

FIGURE 15.—ZOUAVE JACKET (*Queen, 1864*)
White cashmere or cotton piqué braided with black or colour.

From Garibaldi they took his shirt, from the fierce red-stockinged Zouave his jacket" (*Queen*, 1862). The Zouave jacket was a particularly characteristic garment worn between 1859 and 1865, a very short jacket with an open front cut away at the waist (Fig. 15). It was often made in a scarlet woollen fabric, and trimmed with gold braid, black braid or black and white stitching. It was usually worn over a white habit shirt, or a white Garibaldi bodice. Many of the short loose jackets were made in light woollen fabrics such as cashmere, and were used for seaside or very informal wear out of doors and sometimes as indoor jackets.

Heavier woollen materials were a good deal used for winter coats and jackets during the 1860s, far more than they had been earlier in the period (Plate 21).

The three-quarter-length cloak and the short cape were also worn in the late 1850s and during the 1860s, both for day and evening wear. They were now usually circular in form, some with a seam down the centre back. They were made in many different fabrics, and sometimes to match a dress. For evening wear, light soft woollen materials were particularly fashionable. There were many evening cloaks and capes of white cashmere, some trimmed with gold braid or black lace, some lined and trimmed with blue silk. Others were made in the more transparent woollen fabrics and left unlined. Some of these fabrics were woven with silk in striped patterns. Many of the evening cloaks had tasselled hoods.

Although the jackets and cloaks and the circular cloaks and capes were much worn, the mantle never completely disappeared. The cloak forms with open sleeves followed the general style of the earlier mantles, but were now mostly large and shawl-like. Even more shawl-like was the burnous, a fashionable evening mantle of the early 1860s. The name had come into the fashionable vocabulary as early as 1837, when a writer in the *World of Fashion* referred to the "Bernous, imported from Arabia, now naturalized among us". The burnous mantles first bearing this name do not now suggest anything very Arabian, but in the late 1850s, when the burnous was usually made of a folded scarf of cashmere or other woollen fabric sewn together at the back and tasselled to fall like a hood, it had a stronger suggestion of its exotic origin.

The trimming of the loose jackets and capes was often in borders of applied braids or stitching in arabesque patterns, particularly in black on bright or light colours and white on black. Gold on white was much used for evening wraps. Trimming falling from the top of the cloak at the back was characteristic of the 1860s. Many cloaks and capes from the late 1850s and 1860s had borders of quilted silk. In the late 1860s, beaded braid and fringe was popular everywhere as a trimming and appeared on both dresses and outer garments.

In the early 1870s, the cloak and cape forms continued for

evening wear, and the short cape for day wear. The material used for them changed, the lighter woollen fabrics gradually disappearing and poplin and corded silks joining the still popular cashmere. The pleated frills, which were a characteristic trimming of the 1870s, appeared on them and are a mark of this date.

The loose short jacket was still worn in the early 1870s, but now often with fringed trimming, and open below the waist at the centre back. Other short jackets had a pleat down the centre back, usually referred to as a Watteau pleat. This appeared in both jackets and mantles. The form of jacket or coat which was particularly characteristic of the early 1870s was one with a loose straight front and a closely-fitting back, ending in a deep basque. In the shorter jackets the basque was usually open at the centre back, and sometimes also at the sides, forming a short, tabbed, skirt. In the longer coats, the polonaise form of the dress was repeated, a fitted bodice with the skirt puffed at the back over the bustle and open in front. These were usually three-quarter-length. Some of them had the waist defined by a band. They had different forms of sleeve; a fitting, but not tight, sleeve with a cuff, and an open pagoda sleeve were the two main forms.

After 1875, coats shared the changing lines of the dresses and lost their basques and fullness. The fashionable coat-form of the late 1870s was a closely-fitting coat, three-quarter-length or longer, showing a long, continuous line. This line was emphasized by the plainness of many of the coats, which were shaped closely to the figure and buttoned down the front. Some were double-breasted, particularly those made in heavier cloth for travelling wear. These travelling coats, which often had added capes, were long, ending just above the hem of the dress, and were, from this time, often known as ulsters. Sleeves were usually fitting and often cuffed, but some were influenced by the dolman forms of sleeve which were general in the mantles of the 1870s.

The mantles of the early 1870s, like the jackets, often had a pleat at the back. Some with this loose back were slightly fitted in front; others had a fitted back and loose front. They differed from the coats and jackets in having sleeves falling as capes from the shoulder, sometimes falling with longer, hanging ends. In the first half of the decade, those with fitted backs had the basque form of the coats. In the second half, some mantles had the same fitted lines as the coat, but with sleeves cut as capes over the shoulder or as square-ended openings at elbow-length; others had long, hanging ends in front with a cape at the back, an 1870s version of the mantle with scarf-ends.

The mantles generally had more trimming than the coats and jackets. Fringes were the usual trimming throughout the 1870s and, by the end of the decade, beadwork appeared everywhere: "every article for outdoor wear is beaded" (*Ladies' Treasury*, 1880). Fur was used in the traditional way as a trimming for outdoor garments and jackets but in the late 1870s the fashion for coats and jackets entirely of fur was beginning: "The rage of the season . . . is for a sealskin jacket trimmed with otter or beaver" (*Queen*, 1872).

During the 1880s, the mantle was the usual form. The long, slim line of the late 1870s continued for the first years of the decade and the longer mantles generally increased their length, so that often only the hem of the dress was visible beneath. The use of the dolman types of sleeve was general in all these full-length forms, turning the coat into a full-length mantle, fitting in all but the sleeves. From 1883, the slimness of the line broke to take the increasing fullness in the skirt of the dress. The fullness of the evening mantles was given either by pleating, falling from the waist at the centre back, or by the width of the cape-like side sections, gored to a narrow back width. There was sometimes a combination of both these devices in full- or three-quarter-length mantles.

Short mantles were also worn, in great variety, in the 1880s (Plate 22). Some had fitted backs, ending at the bustle, or were a little longer, opening to go over it. They were usually trimmed at this point with a bow of ribbon. The back and front sections were usually narrow and the cape shaping for the arms, full. This form with the wide cape from the shoulder continued to be worn on both long and short mantles, but the short sleeve starting from the elbow was perhaps the more general form for the 1880s. Sleeve shaping which ended at the elbow and revealed the lower half of the arm also appeared in the lighter mantles of this time. From 1885, the sling sleeve, formed by the front section of the mantle being turned up inside to form a sling, was a distinctive fashion. Many of the shorter mantles had their narrow fronts extending into scarf ends.

Short jackets, usually in cloth, were worn as a plainer fashion. Shorter than the fitted jackets of the 1870s, they were made with closely fitting bodice, and basque-shaped with pleating at the back to lie closely over the hips.

There were short capes of two kinds: one was a decorative addition to the costume, light in fabric, but heavily decorated, usually with beads; the other was a short cloth cape, often a double or triple cape, which appeared in the second half of the decade as a driving cape.

A large proportion of the mantles and capes of the 1880s were black. The fabrics used for them were velvet and corded silk, and also the lighter fabrics, net or lace, weighted with bead embroidery. Mantles in bright, rich colours were usually in plush, one of the most characteristic fabrics of the 1880s (Plate 22). The heavier figured silks were also fashionable and appeared in the mantles. Figured materials other than silk were also used, and there are many examples of a woven shawl of earlier fashion being cut up to make a mantle of the 1880s. The weight of the heavier winter mantles was often increased by a quilted lining. The mantles bore a great deal of trimming, chenille fringe, silk fringe, edgings of fur and feathers, lace, braid and beaded braid and embroidery.

From 1884, jackets and mantles of day wear often had a high, fitting band at the neck, like the dresses. At the end of the decade, both the true sleeve of the jackets and the sleeve-shaping of the mantles—which usually included a seam over the shoulder from front to back—rose above the shoulder seam. This high shoulder is a mark of the years 1889 to 1892 and was followed by the swelling out of the sleeve into the full leg-of-mutton sleeve of the mid-1890s worn from 1893 to 1897. Another distinctive mark of this decade in its outer garments was a high collar, often as high as the ears, standing out from the neck (Plate 23), sometimes lined with feathers or ruched silk.

The mantle forms of the 1880s continued in wear until about 1892; but they were already passing out of fashion by 1890, except in one or two forms which occasionally appeared as variants of the cape during the 1890s.

The short, full circular cape was perhaps more worn than any other outer garment of the 1890s, although it became a dominant fashion only with the rise of the full sleeve in 1893. It appeared on all occasions and may be found in many different fabrics. It was worn as an evening wrap, in silks, trimmed with feathers, fur and beading. For day wear it appeared in the smooth-surfaced face-cloth that had now become popular as a "ladies' cloth", plain or with trimmings of braid or patterned appliqué of cloth (Plate 23). For travel and sporting wear there were capes of tweed, often lined with brightly coloured plaids and sometimes with an additional cape and hood. The evening and dress capes usually had the full circular collar, which is like an inverted miniature of the cape itself. The tweed capes usually had a smaller, square-ended collar.

Full-length cloaks were also worn throughout the 1890s. At first they fell, with high shoulder line, rather slim and straight, often from a square yoke, but by 1893 they showed a greater fullness, to take the full sleeves beneath. The fullness was given often by a double pleat falling from the neck or yoke at the centre back. This pleating is found on cloaks, coats and jackets to the end of the century. It is a reappearance of the shaping that was occasionally used in the 1870s. Once again it was often called a Watteau pleat. It derived from a construction used over a long period of the eighteenth century, but never then known by this name. By the end of the century another, less enveloping form of cloak appeared, with the fronts cut in a curving line to reveal part of the gown beneath.

A full-length coat was also worn for both day and evening wear during the 1890s. The early 1890s coat was usually a plain fitted form with a high sleeve and a high shoulder line. After 1893, the fitted form continued, with the sleeve widened to take the full sleeves of the dress; but a yoked form, with the fullness falling from a central pleat, like the cloaks, was more general. After 1897, the sleeve was once more close to the arm. By the end of the century, it was becoming wider at the opening. At the same time, the fronts of the curved coats open to a wider line at the hem.

The fitted form was much worn in three-quarter-length coats and also in the jackets which ended at the waist or in a short basque below it. The jacket was a popular fashion for day-time wear. It was worn with a skirt or dress, either matching or contrasting in colour and material. It appeared in both single and double-breasted forms. Loose jackets with yokes were also worn in the second half of the decade. Like the capes, the short jackets had great range of wear and were made in many materials from tweed to velvet, with elaborate trimmings of lace and embroidery or braidings. Very short jackets, not unlike the "Zouave" jackets of the 1860s—a name sometimes used again, although they were now usually called boleros—appeared in the late 1890s. Their curving lines repeated the line then appearing at the lower edge of most of the outer garments of this time.

The cape form was so dominant a fashion that short capes appeared on coats and three-quarter-length jackets, and often the trimming which was added to the necks of many of the more elaborate cloaks, capes, coats and jackets—in ruches and pleated frills of chiffon or lace—showed a cape-like form. On the jackets the revers were often large and emphasized by decoration or the use of contrasting material. They were often elaborately braided and were sometimes worn with a matching vest. Evening cloaks, coats and capes showed an increasing richness and elaboration in fabric and trimming. In the second half of the decade, the linings also became very elaborate, and this concentration of ornament on a lining is seen again in the parasols of these last years of the century.

Victorian shawls were made in almost every known material, in every technique of textile construction. Their ornament was part of their making, or was added in embroidery and trimming. They were gathered or received influence from many countries of the world.

During the first half of the period, between 1837 and 1870, the shawl was one of the most fashionable of outdoor coverings. Squares or approximate squares, the double square and a square cut across the diagonal forming a triangle but without more shaping, are here all included as shawls, and the term scarf is given to those in which the length is more than double the width.

The scarf had been the more fashionable shape early in the century and, up to 1830, square shawls were rather small, about one and a half yards square. Scarves were still being worn in the late 1830s and 1840s as summer wraps, but after the middle of the century they were less often fashionable, even for summer wearing. The size of shawls increased to a square of about sixty-four inches in the 1840s, and in the 1850s and 1860s shawls two yards square, and the double square of sixty-four inches by a hundred and twenty-eight or more, were worn over the spreading skirts. This increasing size is no final guide to date, but only a guide to the basic movement of fashion between 1840 and 1870.

The most prized of Victorian shawls are those of intricately woven pattern usually called Paisley shawls, but often examples of wool or cotton printed in bright colours with the same cone design are undeservedly prized, because "Paisley" has become synonymous with this ubiquitous nineteenth-century pattern. The Paisley shawl has an Indian origin, and the Indian shawls which were its prototype were also brought to this country from the beginning of the nineteenth century.

The shawl of Indian origin which remains an Indian shawl without European versions is a shawl of twilled wool, composed of many smaller pieces, embroidered separately, in bright coloured wools, and then sewn together. These shawls were made throughout the century and prized in Victorian England, but they were a nineteenth-century innovation in India to supply a cheaper version of the traditional woven shawl.

This Indian shawl, which exerted a widespread influence in European fashion, was a shawl woven of goats' wool in characteristic patterns. The development of the Indian shawl and its characteristic cone design, and the relations of the Indian, French and English shawl industries, have been fully dealt with and well illustrated in John Irwin's excellent monograph, *Shawls*.

At the beginning of Victoria's reign, shawls and scarves were imported from India; shawls of Indian pattern were imported from France; and similar shawls were being made in Britain at Norwich and Paisley. The Indian shawls were of fine goat-wool. The earlier versions made in this country were woven of silk and fine wool in a twill pattern, but, by the 1830s, fine wool, a substitute for the Indian goat-fleece, was being used for them. A shawl woven in silk and wool twill, with patterned borders sewn on and not woven in one piece, is likely to be earlier than 1840. Scarves may have deep patterned borders at the ends, woven in one piece, and narrow sewn-on borders. In most shawls and scarves earlier than 1840, the pattern is limited to the border and the centre is left plain. Some shawls may have this centre covered with a small repeating design, but the closely patterned area remains limited to the borders. Cream was the usual colour for the ground, but in the 1830s many shawls were patterned in vivid colours against a black ground. The formalized cone design was the characteristic feature of nineteenth-century Indian, French and Paisley shawls; but it does not appear on every example.

During the 1840s, as the larger shawls grew more fashionable, the patterning of them grew richer, the borders deepening until, by 1850, the pattern covered the whole area of the shawl. A fine shawl was at this time a much-prized, much-desired acquisition. "Shawls were never more in favour than during the present winter. To say nothing of the products of the Indian looms or the highly and deservedly prized French cashmere, some of the newest specimens of our own British manufacture will find favour. . . . To say which is the favourite colour for a shawl would be impossible, for the ground is completely covered by a rich mass of intricate and varied arabesques presenting an effect perfectly oriental" (*Lady's Newspaper*, 1847).

The fashion continued throughout the 1850s, was declining in the 1860s and died out by about 1870. A reversible shawl, without a wrong side, the pattern identical on both sides, was introduced just at the end of the shawl's period of fashion in the late 1860s. Many of the finer shawls were too much prized to be discarded and some appear again in new forms in the mantles of the 1870s and 1880s. "It seems a pity to cut up a valuable shawl to make a dolman, but such is being done now" (*Ladies' Treasury*, 1880). There was still occasional use of them in their original form; a writer in the *Queen* in 1881 referred to a "long India shawl draped in a new manner". Shawls of woven pattern of the mid-nineteenth century, Indian, French or Paisley, survive in hundreds still, evidence of a dominant nineteenth-century fashion.

The woven shawls were expensive. Cheaper imitations were printed with the same designs on wool, wool and cotton, or cotton fabrics. There were also printed shawls of finer quality, shawls of silk, or silk and wool, in gauze weave with the pattern printed in rich jewel-like colours. Many of these are the large rectangular shawls approximately five feet by ten feet.

In the 1830s, shawls of silk crêpe, plain, embroidered, or with printed designs, were worn, and embroidered Chinese crêpe shawls continued to be fashionable during the 1840s. Shawls of printed satin were also fashionable at the beginning of the period. Twilled silk—levantine—a material much used in the 1820s, was still used for shawls and scarves in the 1830s, plain or with figured patterns, but it is not often found in them after the 1840s. The 1830s fashion for bright colours against a dark ground appears in shawls of all kinds.

Shawls and scarves usually have fringed ends or borders. The fringes are of different kinds. The plainest is the fringe of warp threads left at each end. There is the simple knotting of these threads, and the more elaborate knotting into two or three lines of mesh. Other fringes are knotted on to the ends or borders, strands of silk or wool being threaded through the edge of the material and then knotted. Or there is fringed braid which is sewn on.

Changeable or shot silk appears in shawls of the 1840s, and many shawls and scarves were made in the light, half-transparent woollen fabrics also fashionable at this time. Many light shawls and scarves survive of silk, wool, or a mixture of silk and wool, in gauze weave, or open weave, with striped borders of silk in a single bright colour. Mainly from their colours, they suggest a period of wear between about 1840 and 1865. Some of these may have been shawls made to match a dress, which was a fashion of the early 1860s. Shawls and scarves of tartan stripes in silk and satin are also likely to date from the 1860s.

The white embroidered muslin which appeared everywhere in the costume of the 1830s and 1840s appeared also in shawls. Shawls of embroidered muslin were square or triangular, but a long scarf form in embroidered muslin seems to have been little worn. The shawls show the same patterns as other embroidered muslin accessories. Sometimes they are finished with a muslin frill with a scalloped edge, sometimes with an edging of bobbin lace. A number of them are lined with silk in pale colours.

Knitting in delicate openwork patterns in fine white wool, as practised in the Shetland Islands, became fashionable for shawls in the 1840s, and patterns for knitting them and other accessories are often given in fashion journals, particularly between 1847 and 1850.

Black shawls were also worn in the 1830s and 1840s, in silk, satin, and corded silk, often edged with lace, particularly black silk bobbin lace. There were also black shawls of lace, usually either bobbin lace or machine net, embroidered in black silk. There was a revival of netting in black silk, and hand-netted shawls and scarves were fashionable summer wear from the beginning of the reign until about 1850.

Black lace shawls were much worn in the late 1850s and early 1860s when the mingling of black lace and light silk was a fashionable contrast. The finest of them are of silk bobbin lace, usually Chantilly, whose still graceful patterns and clear ground were displayed to perfection over the wide unbroken spread of light silk in a skirt of the 1860s. Others were in black silk Maltese bobbin lace and black silk machine lace. They were made either as squares or triangles, the squares usually two yards square to two and a half yards, the triangles with a diagonal of about three yards.

The lace shawls were the lighter shawls of summer wear. The contrast of black lace and light material was repeated in the warmer shawls of fine twilled wool, known as cashmere, white, grey or fawn, which were trimmed with black lace, or sometimes embroidered in black silk and beads. Shawls of scarlet cashmere with black lace trimming are likely also to belong to the 1860s, when the combination of bright scarlet and black and white appeared constantly in women's dress. Black shawls in the same fabric, embroidered in black silk and lace-trimmed, were also worn during the 1860s.

Woollen shawls, woven in check patterns, about a yard and three-quarters square, were worn throughout the nineteenth century. They were, for most of the time, worn below the level of fashion. The type can still be seen occasionally in actual wear in the streets of industrial towns of North-west England.

CHAPTER 8

HATS AND BONNETS

THE bonnet which was worn in the year of Queen Victoria's accession had a wide brim, not so large as it had been in the 1830s, but still making a wide spreading frame for the face. The crown, which was roughly the shape of a cone with the top cut off, was set at an angle to the brim. This was the shape for bonnets of straw and for those made of silk or velvet on a stiff foundation (Plate 24); but there was another method of making which gave a slightly different shaping. The drawn bonnets, those in which the material was gathered over a framework of cane or wire, had the same shaping of the brim, but the framework gave a horseshoe shape to the puffed and gathered crown.

The straw bonnets may be Leghorn bonnets, that is, of straw grown in Tuscany and plaited in the Italian fashion. These were still the most fashionable of straw bonnets. They can be distinguished by the fineness of the straw, and by the method of plaiting, with each braid plaited into the next so that the fabric of the bonnet appears continuous. Their English rivals, rather less fashionable and expensive, were Dunstable bonnets of English straw, in which the larger English wheat-straw was split before plaiting and the plaited braids were then sewn together. In some bonnets the Leghorn straw was used, plaited and sewn in England in the English manner.

Straw bonnets were worn during the summer months. They were worn fashionably with walking dress, but amongst the less fashionable and in the country they appeared on all occasions. These bonnets were nearly always plainly trimmed, with ribbons. The more fashionable dress bonnets were in silk of many different kinds, plain silk or satin, watered silk, figured silk; and transparent bonnets in net, crêpe or lace were regarded as specially becoming. Velvet was the usual material for winter.

Ribbon and feathers were the most general trimming; the bird of paradise plume was the most fashionable for the years 1835 to 1845. Flowers were also used. The trimming of the inside of the brim was as important as the trimming of the outside of the bonnet, and lace, ribbon and flowers were used to ornament it. The lining of the bonnet brim was also important. "No one article in the whole range of female costume is more important in its effects than that comparatively small piece of satin, silk or other material that forms the lining of the bonnet" (Mrs. M. J. Howell, *Handbook of Millinery*, 1847). But some straw bonnets appear to have been worn with unlined brims. The bonnets mostly have wide ribbons to tie beneath the chin, and a curtain— which in the straw bonnets may be of straw or ribbon—to shield the back of the neck. The curtain—or *bavolet*, for it is sometimes called by its French name—is found in almost all bonnets from the beginning of the period until the 1860s (Plate 24).

Straw bonnets of this early period may be found now, either denuded of their original ribbons and feathers or with the added trimmings of "dressing up", professional or amateur. The straw ones are more likely to have suffered alteration than the silk ones, where trimming and foundation can less easily be separated, but any bonnet may, of course, have had flowers, ribbons and feathers removed from it or added to it.

The change in the shape of the bonnet began in 1838, when a form with brim and crown continuous in a straight line appeared (Plate 24). This was not a new form. Bonnets of this type, which had been known as the cottage bonnet, had been worn in the first decade of the century. The shaping of the 1840s was distinguished from the earlier examples by the downward curve of the lower edge from the back of the crown to the edge of the brim, the brim coming down low on the cheek, covering the face. For the whole of the next decade, 1840 to 1850, this was the bonnet form. The only variation was in its close and open styles, the former closing in on the face and the latter having a wider brim; but both, in profile, had the same horizontal line from brim to crown.

The drawn-bonnet construction of the 1830s continued in this new form. Silk or satin was gathered over a series of cane hoops, and the back of the crown was a stiffened circle (Plate 24). Other bonnets were made in silk and satin, laid tightly over a stiff foundation. Straw bonnets still continued to be worn for summer. Chip plait, which is made from fine wood splints, was also fashionable. From the middle of the 1840s, openwork straw plaits, and fine straw mixed with horsehair in fancy braids, or alternate braids of straw and horsehair, were much used (Plate 24). Velvet remained the usual material for winter bonnets.

The trimming was ribbon, a wreath of flowers or a single feather falling from the centre down one side of the bonnet. There was still trimming inside the brim—a ruching of ribbon, net or lace, a wreath of flowers to frame the face, or knots of ribbon, net or lace, or flowers at each side (Plate 3).

By 1850 the open form of bonnet was more general than the close, and from this came the change of bonnet shape in the 1850s. The brim opened more widely round the face and the crown grew lower and smaller, so that by 1853 the new shaping was established: "it is the peculiar form of crown which gives this appearance, by being made low and sloping towards the back" (*World of Fashion*, 1853). This bonnet was worn well back on the head, revealing the face, looking a little as if it were slipping off backwards (Plate 3). Bonnets of the last two years of the decade have the sides curving back, exposing yet more of the face, but the top more forward on the forehead. In the early 1860s, the front rose high, narrow and rather pointed, with the sides receding, giving a shape which was aptly called spoon-shaped. Straw, horsehair, velvet, net and crêpe were all fashionable for these bonnets, and they were trimmed with flowers, feathers, ribbon and lace. They usually had very long curtains in the late 1850s and early 1860s. "The *bavolet* has remained stationary. Had it increased in size, it would have become quite a tippet" (*Ladies' Treasury*, 1858).

At the beginning of the reign, hats were not fashionable, although by the late 1840s a large, round straw hat was being worn at the seaside, and for garden and country wear. These hats were usually rather flat-crowned with wide, turned-down brims, made of coarse straw (Plate 20). From 1857, hats became fashionable wear for younger women: "of course they are not suited to elderly ladies" (*World of Fashion*, 1857). These also were hats with

24. Bonnets, 1835–58

(above) *Cream silk on a stiff foundation with a cone-shaped crown set at
an angle to the wide brim, the style of
the beginning of the reign, 1835–8.*
(below, left) *Split straw and horsehair plait, the brim and crown still in a
straight line, but a line sloping now
towards the back of the head, the
style of 1853–8.*
(below right) *Shot silk, cream and
red, gathered over a framework of
cane, the brim and crown in a straight
line, the style of 1840–50. All have
the curtain at the back of the crown
to shade the neck.*

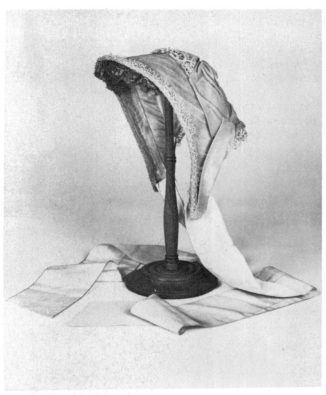

25.   Hat and bonnet, 1865–70

(left)   *Bonnet of white horsehair braids trimmed with bobbin lace, mauve ribbon and flowers beneath the brim, worn flat on top of the head resting on a large chignon, 1865–70.*

(right)   *Hat of Leghorn straw plait trimmed with blue ribbon and lace, the brim edged with blue velvet. This is a narrower version of the style which appeared for informal wear in the late 1850s (see Plate 3), worn in the late 1860s with a forward tilt.*

26.   Hat and bonnets, 1875–90

(right)   *Hat of grey-green fibre braids, the brim lined with dull green velvet, trimmed with cream velvet, lace and roses. This is the* postboy *shape of 1884–8.*

(below, left) *Bonnet of fawn fibre braids trimmed with darker feather, ribbon in two shades of fawn, and lace, worn high on the head, 1875–7.*

(below right) *Bonnet of navy blue and red straw plait, trimmed with red-bordered blue velvet ribbon and red wing feathers which arch at the centre front of the bonnet, a characteristic trimming 1887–9.*

rather flat crowns, but wide curving brims, a form usually trimmed with ribbon and feathers placed at the front (Plate 3). Hats were still only used for the most informal wear but, during the 1860s, hats of different shapes were gradually taking the place of bonnets —at least for the younger women—for all but the most formal occasions (Plate 5). In 1861, there were three main shapes: a hat with oval crown and brim turned up at the sides (Plate 25); a round hat with turned back brim (Plate 5); and a higher-crowned bell-shaped hat. A small sailor hat with round crown and straight narrow brim joined these shapes in 1863. This, and the round hat with the turned-back brim, were the hats of children before they were adopted for adult fashion. From 1863, for the next three or four years, two other shapes were much worn: a high-crowned hat with a narrow brim flat all round and a hat with a slightly lower crown and the brim turned up each side but down at back and front. The Tyrolean hat, a fashion of the last year of the decade and worn for a year or two, was another version of the high-crowned hat, with scarcely any brim at all.

An important innovation at this time was the use of felt for fashionable hats. It was not a new material for women's hats, for it had been used in the eighteenth century and for nineteenth-century riding hats, but it had only rarely appeared amongst the fashionable bonnet forms of the 1830s, 1840s and 1850s. It came into general fashionable use only with the revival of the hat, from the late 1850s onwards. Summer hats were made of straw and horsehair plait, winter ones of felt and velvet. The trimming of hats was usually fairly restrained; ribbon, particularly velvet ribbon was most used and often the edge of the brim was bound with it (Plate 25). Feathers were often added to this in hats of the late 1850s and early 1860s; after 1863, flowers appear on hats as well as on bonnets. The trimming was most often placed at the front.

Many bonnets of the 1860s are difficult to distinguish from dress caps of the same time. In 1863, the high raised front flattened, the crown grew smaller, and the sides, which were already receding, disappeared; at the same time the curtain grew smaller and then also disappeared. By the mid-1860s, the bonnet was no more than a light shell of horsehair or crêpe, high on the back of the head (Plate 25)—"no longer bonnets but plaques of lace trimmed with the tiniest of flowers" (*Ladies' Treasury*, 1866). These very small bonnets continued in fashion until 1870, when the fashion journals were still making the same comment: "no such thing as a bonnet is now in existence, and what is so called is a mere ornament for the head—a puff, a diadem, a lace fluting, a bonnet of flowers, a band of ribbon" (*Englishwoman's Domestic Magazine*, 1870).

The changing styles of hat and bonnet during the 1860s were closely linked with the changing fashion in hairdressing. During the 1860s, the chignon increased in size and rose from a position low at the back of the head in the first half of the decade to a mass of hair high at the back of the head by the end of it, a change which makes it clear that the bonnet of the early 1860s could no longer be worn in the late 1860s. The strings of the small flat bonnets were often tied at the back beneath this high chignon. Roughly speaking, the size of the bonnet in the late 1860s was in inverse proportion to the quantity of hair, whether real or added, displayed in the hairdressing. The raising of the hairdressing at the back of the head meant that, from 1867, hats were worn tilted forward over the forehead: the small bonnets rested flat at the top of the head or made a narrow diadem of crêpe or lace with flowers or ribbon at the front of the head.

From 1871, the hairdressing became looser, but still more complicated and elaborate, usually needing much additional hair. High-crowned hats, with turned-up brims, continued to be worn, tilted over the forehead, and these were perhaps the most popular form of the early 1870s. From 1872 a new form appeared. This was a hat like a boy's sailor hat of the time, with a round crown, and brim turned up all round. It was much worn and remained fashionable until 1875. "The round *marin anglais* hat with sloped-up brim all round which ladies wear pushed over chignons . . . is certainly the most absurd fashion . . . yet it is a great favourite with ladies of almost all ages. These chapeaus are exactly the same shape as our little boys' felt hats . . . only they are ornamented with feathers and aigrettes and tied with broad strings of grosgrain or moiré ribbon" (*Englishwoman's Domestic Magazine*, 1875).

From 1872, and more generally from 1873, the high chignon

was worn inside the crowns of hats and bonnets, so that the forward tilt changed to a backward tilt for bonnets, and hats rested high on top of the head (Plate 6). The round brimmed hat was also worn in a bonnet form, the only difference being the strings which tied the bonnet under the chin. Then even this slight distinction was lost for a few years in the mid-1870s, when bonnets were worn without strings. The flat bonnets of the 1860s had disappeared, but the diadem form, without crown but profusely trimmed with flowers, remained. From 1874, the upturned brims of the sailor bonnet were trimmed with flowers. A bonnet with a round crown, like this, but with a diadem form in front, was another style of the mid-1870s. By 1877, wide strings which tied in a bow under the chin once again appeared on the bonnet. The bonnet with diadem brim remained popular and another form—usually called the Directoire—which has the brim lowered so that it lies flat, close to but not touching the head, was also popular (Plate 26). By the end of the decade, bonnets resembling hats had given place to a more definite bonnet form; the brim disappeared from the back and wide strings were once more tied beneath the chin.

The high-crowned hat disappeared in the mid-1870s, although versions of this form with lower, less sharply defined crowns were still being worn until the end of the decade. A new hat form for the second half of the 1870s was one with a larger crown and a medium brim which turned up at the back. A toque shape with a fairly high crown also became fashionable from 1877, and was worn resting high on the head. From 1878, a round crowned hat with wide brim turned up at one side, known as the Gainsborough, was worn and continued as a popular fashion into the 1880s.

Hats of the 1870s were more elaborately trimmed than hats of the 1860s. In the early years of the decade, both bonnets and hats were often trimmed with ribbons at the back, which hung over the chignon, in addition to other trimming. These disappeared in 1875. After 1874, bonnets showed an increasing use of flowers in their trimming. "Simple field blossoms are the most fashionable this summer," said the *Englishwoman's Domestic Magazine* in 1875, but almost any kind of flowers may be found on them. The same journal commented in the following year that drooping foliage was worn; "a pleasant relief from the stiffness of the bonnets worn two years ago with high brim and formal flowers". In the second half of the 1870s, and in the 1880s, whole birds as well as parts of birds were used for the trimming of bonnets. Feathers were much used in the millinery of the 1880s, not only as trimmings but also as the fabric of the whole hat, particularly in the toque forms. Plush, a favourite fabric of the 1880s, was also much used for winter millinery, as it was for dresses, muffs and bags. The earlier materials, velvet, felt, straw, all continued in use; but silk was not much used, apart from the light crêpe of the much-trimmed dress bonnets. Lace was used as part of the fabric of the lighter bonnets, mingled with flowers and feathers. Beaver appeared again from 1887. Straw hats and bonnets were much worn throughout the 1880s, when they lost their seasonal connection and appeared amongst winter as well as summer fashions. "Throughout the year, straw is the one material that never goes out and vast numbers of straw bonnets are made with rows of velvet alternating with the straw" (*Woman's World*, 1888). The coarser straw plaits (Plate 10) were fashionable and fancy straw plaits in openwork patterns appeared again in the 1880s, but the openwork plaits of this period are heavier and less lace-like than the earlier openwork plaits of the 1850s.

The large hat with one side turned up, the Gainsborough, remained fashionable for almost the whole of the 1880s. From 1884, a new style of hat appeared, which was particularly characteristic of the 1880s, although the fashion journals insisted at first that it was a style suitable only to very young faces. This was the postilion or post-boy hat, with high crown like a flowerpot, and narrow brim. Hats with this shaping of the crown were fashionable between 1884 and 1888 (Plate 26). Some had a fairly narrow brim turned up at one side; some had the brim turned up at the back and straight in the front, a style called Directoire although it bore little resemblance to the bonnet which had been given that name a few years earlier; on others, the brim was turned back at each side. The high crown also appeared in the toque, with a wide banded brim. In 1888, "The hats which are distinctively new have brims that widen in front and more closely resemble the sailor shape than any other. Some of these brims turn upwards like an inverted saucer" (*Woman's World*, 1888). This style of hat with the brim jutting out over the face was a characteristic fashion of the years from 1888 to 1892. Hats of the sailor shape, either with a high crown and a broad flat brim or with a flatter crown and medium brim, were "worn by the million" in 1887 (Plate 10). Severely plain versions of this shape, in stiffened straw with a ribbon band, were worn for yachting and tennis and, by 1890, hats in this style had become generally worn, not only for all summer sports but with the plainer and more practical styles of everyday dress (Fig. 16).

FIGURE 16.—SAILOR AND BOAT-SHAPED HATS (*Lady, 1894*)
(*Left*) Sailor hat in costume drill or fine straw; (*Centre*) The boat shape;
(*Right*) Sailor hat trimmed with silk ribbon.

In bonnets the style of 1880 continued until 1884. During the mid-1880s, bonnet crowns also grew higher, though less noticeably than those of hats. Brims often made a pointed shape over the forehead from 1887. A fashion for bonnets without strings, which came again in 1888, makes it difficult to distinguish between a bonnet and a toque of this date. The toque was a fashion for younger women, who also wore the very small bonnets without crowns which were once again fashionable by 1888. Particularly characteristic of the bonnets of the early 1880s was the edging of the bonnet brim with beads. The strings of the bonnets at this time were wide. Ribbons, feathers and flowers were all used as trimmings. In 1888 it was said that "nothing in flowers is *à la mode* unless it looks as if it had just been gathered in the garden and tied up loosely", and that "fashionable hats all resemble walking gardens" (*Woman's World*, 1888). Lace was often used to trim straw bonnets and hats, as well as being used with plush and velvet. The brims of straw bonnets and hats of this decade were often lined with velvet (Plate 26), and hats of the late 1880s sometimes had trimming beneath the brim. For hats of more informal wear, silk scarves were used as trimming, loosely knotted round the crown.

The arrangement of the trimming is a distinguishing mark of hats and bonnets of the second half of the decade. From 1885, it

FIGURE 17.—HAT, TOQUE AND BONNET (*Lady, 1894*)
(*Left*) Hat with velvet crown and straw brim, trimmed with roses and lace;
(*Centre*) Toque of silk velvet with crown of foliage; (*Right*) Straw bonnet
with loops of lace-trimmed velvet and roses.

was usually arranged with a pointed or arched effect in front and, when the high crown was passing out of fashion in 1888, there was still the effect of height in the stiff bows and feathers of the trimming: "Bonnets, as the months creep on, are not quite so high, though the ribbon bows with which they are trimmed are made to stand up boldly" (*Woman's World*, 1888). Wings of birds were often arched at the front (Plate 26), giving both a pointed effect and height.

By 1890, the bonnets were very small, often almost non-existent, or hidden beneath their trimmings of bows or ribbon, flowers, feathers and lace. The difference between a bonnet and toque of this time was marked only by the strings of the bonnet, now narrow—an inch wide or less—and fixed well at the back (Fig. 17).

By the end of the century, the bonnet with strings had become a middle-aged fashion.

The hats of the 1890s show great variety of shape and size. After 1892 the hat with the brim jutting widely over the face in front went out of fashion. Wide-brimmed hats were still worn, with the brim turned up sometimes at one side, sometimes at both sides, so that the under brim was visible. From the mid-1890s, these wide-brimmed hats were worn placed slightly sideways. The still popular sailor shapes, with flat crowns and straight brims of medium width, were worn straight on the head. Witch-crowned hats, that is, hats with crowns pointed in a cone-shape, were fashionable in the mid-1890s. A crown called "yeoman", which widened at the top, was fashionable in 1896, and another very characteristic crown of this year was the hour-glass crown. The boat-shape, with brim turned up at the sides, still remained a popular fashion, particularly made in felt as a walking or cycling hat (Fig. 16). In 1896 a high-crowned version of this style with the crown cloven, a little like a man's trilby hat, came into fashion. A cloven-crowned hat with flat brim was also worn. Hats with wide brims upturned in front appeared in 1898. If the brim was not upturned, it now often had a curving tilted line from left to right, or was curved up on each side from the centre.

Toques with high crowns were worn in the mid-1890s, and three-pointed or four-pointed toques were also a fashion of these years. By the last years of the century, the toque was larger, with a soft, full crown, and often with a wide turned-back brim and high trimming.

The openwork straws which had been fashionable in the 1880s continued to be worn in the 1890s. Straw, chip, velvet and felt were the chief materials used for hats and bonnets but, for the lighter summer millinery, net, chiffon and lace were often used. Flowers were still used in large quantities for trimming: "Hats continue to look like flower-gardens" (*Woman at Home*, 1896). Violets were particularly fashionable in 1890, and bunches of currants were another favourite trimming of this year. Throughout the decade there was a fashion for a single high ornament in the trimming, an aigrette of lace or ribbon, a high cock's feather, or one or two ostrich plumes (Fig. 17).

Bonnet Veils

Bonnet veils were worn in part as a protection against sun and dirt, in part as an added elegance for the bonnet and head. Those worn in the 1830s were particularly decorative. Many examples of them survive, but they are not always recognized as bonnet veils. They are large, for wearing with the wide-brimmed bonnets, about a yard square, though usually not an exact square; along one side there is a hem to take a drawstring of narrow silk ribbon, and the other sides have a bordering pattern. They are, understandably, often mistaken for aprons. They were made in blonde lace, in machine-made net with embroidered patterns, or in figured silk gauze. Often the ground was patterned within the border. They were white, cream, pale pink or mauve, but during the 1830s there was a very large proportion of black veils. Plain dark blue and green gauze veils were also regarded as suitable for country wear, when protection from the sun rather than decoration was the main concern. Large veils were worn until the mid-1840s, but they then became about half their former size. By 1860, a semicircular bonnet veil was the usual form, just large enough to reach the chin (Plate 3), and black was once again popular. Veils were less worn with the hats of the 1870s and 1880s, but they became more fashionable and larger in the 1890s. The veils of this period were usually clear net, with small spot patterns (Plate 40).

"Uglies"

Another, less decorative, protection from the sun, was used in the 1840s and 1850s. This was a narrow shade, four half-hoops of cane, with silk, usually blue, gathered over them so that it folded into a single half-hoop. It was worn on the front of the bonnet, the two ends tying together beneath the chin. It was known as an "ugly" and was seen mainly at the seaside, where it made an amusing miniature of the hoods which were attached to bathing machines to conceal the bathers' entry into the water.

CHAPTER 9

CAPS AND HEADDRESSES

THE Victorian age has left behind it not only the hats and bonnets worn out of doors, but a great variety of caps and headdresses, some of them in forms which now to an unpractised eye are hardly recognizable as caps. At some periods during the reign, a cap was worn by almost every woman for almost every occasion, at other periods by some women on some occasions, at yet others by a few women only. The caps fall into three main groups: night caps; caps worn with morning and home dress; and the decorative caps of dress wear.

Night caps, which were worn up to about 1880, are almost all rather plain. They were usually of the close bonnet shape to cover the head, with a drawstring across the back, and their shape changed only slightly between 1835 and 1870 (Fig. 20). Most of them were made of lawn or muslin, very often at the beginning of the period in a checkered weave. Some, particularly in the 1840s and 1850s, were knitted in fine cotton, or crocheted. Those in lawn or muslin had frills and strings of a little finer material, and sometimes a narrow insertion of openwork embroidery or a narrow lace edging. The caps of the late 1830s were larger than those of the 1850s and 1860s. By the 1870s, the fashionable night cap had a fuller crown and was no longer a fitting bonnet.

The distinction between night caps and morning caps of the plainer kind worn during the 1840s and 1850s is rather slight. Plainer examples of morning caps of this period not only resemble the night caps of their own time, but also night caps of rather later date. They were also common to different social levels. The *Workwoman's Guide* of 1838 gives the pattern for a cap which is said to be suitable for a "day cap for servants or night cap for any age or station". The more elaborate morning caps made of net or lace, with lace-trimmed frills and insertions of lace and embroidery, present no difficulty, but it is often difficult to decide at what hour in the morning plainer examples in muslin or lawn might have ceased to be worn. The lawn or muslin of morning caps is usually finer and clearer than the fabric of the night caps. They are trimmed with lace and insertions of the fashionable white embroidery. The narrow bobbin laces, now referred to as thread lace, were superseding "blonde", the silk bobbin lace, in morning caps at the beginning of the period. Morning caps usually

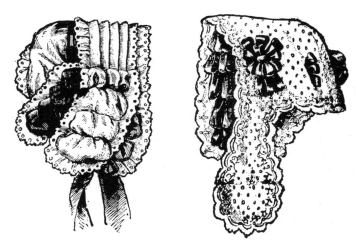

FIGURE 18.—CAPS (*Lady's Newspaper, 1849*)
(*Left*) Morning cap of muslin with embroidered edging and blue ribbon trimming; (*Right*) Cap suitable for dinner dress in the fanchon or half-handkerchief form in Honiton lace and geranium ribbon.

lack the long plain strings of muslin or lawn found on the night caps. A great many of the morning caps were not tied beneath the chin or, if they were, it was by the cap ribbons, which were coloured or patterned ribbons of silk or gauze (Fig. 18). Surviving caps have often lost their ornamental ribbons, which were added to them in bows, rosettes and hanging lappets.

Caps shared the changing lines of the bonnet. Caps of 1837 were still round, and worn high at the back of the head, with their frills making a wide frame for the face. By 1840, they were shaped to cover the ears and lie closer to the head.

During the 1850s, the morning caps grew smaller; like the bonnets, they covered less of the head, starting farther back.

The lighter materials, lace and net and worked muslin, were nearly always used for them (Fig. 20). In the late 1850s, once again following the bonnets, they often had a deep curtain. Caps of alternate bands of Valenciennes lace and insertions of embroidery were fashionable morning wear at the end of the decade. Small round caps netted or crocheted in cotton, with long lappets

FIGURE 19.—CAPS (*Queen*, *1868*)
(*Left*) Morning cap of Cluny lace with trellis of black velvet; (*Right*) Afternoon cap of Valenciennes lace, strings barred with satin ribbon.

over the ears, were made and worn. Other caps were made of a long strip of crochet or lace or embroidered muslin which lay over the head, covering the ears and falling to the shoulders. By 1860 the form of cap known as a fanchon had become much worn as a morning cap. This was a small, roughly triangular piece of muslin, which rested on top of the head with long streamers of muslin falling behind. Another version of this was a small square of lace or embroidered muslin with the point worn in the centre of the forehead and long bows and ends at the back. These caps did not cover the large chignon of hair but rested on it

(Fig. 19). Another type of cap which was fashionable from 1862
was a cap with an oval caul of muslin, enclosing the hair, often

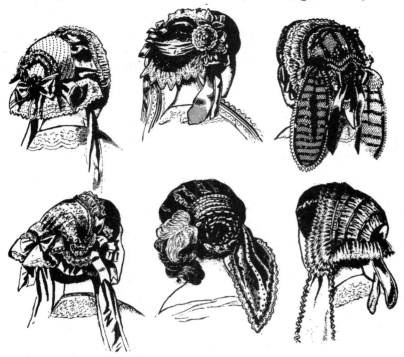

FIGURE 20.—CAPS (*World of Fashion, 1857*)
(*Top, left to right*): Morning cap, spotted net and lace, blue ribbons.
Evening cap of net, lace, ribbon and roses. Morning cap, net, lace, velvet
and ribbon, with lappets.
(*Bottom, left to right*): Embroidered muslin cap trimmed lace and green satin
ribbon. Evening headdress crimson gauze, blond lace and white feather.
Night cap of cambric, worked at edge.

called a Charlotte Corday cap. This remained fashionable during
the 1860s; and the name persisted for a muslin cap with a soft,
full crown in the mid-1870s, although at this time the fullness
came higher on the head, with long streamers and a bow at the
back, following the changing styles of hairdressing. The small
squares with lappets and streamers also continued in use as
morning caps during the 1870s. Their wide strings of lace or
lace-trimmed muslin were often brought in front and fastened
loosely beneath the chin in the late 1860s and early 1870s. The

fine twilled wool, known as cashmere, a material much used in the 1860s, was sometimes used for morning caps at this time, and caps of knitted wool were also worn. After 1880 the wearing of morning caps by younger women was limited to breakfast time and then ceased altogether.

The more elaborate morning caps of net or lace passed without sharp distinction into dress caps of the plainer kind. Morning caps, apart from their ribbons, were usually white or pale cream; the dress caps, although they might also be white, usually showed greater use of colour. Like the morning caps, dress caps proper also showed the changing lines of the bonnet; if some dress caps are not greatly different from morning caps, others are not very different from the lighter versions of the bonnet.

The close-fitting style, which had developed for bonnets and caps by 1840, remained as one of the styles in dress caps of the 1840s and early 1850s. These dress caps were small, light bonnets usually made of lace, net or silk gauze. At the beginning of the period, "blonde" lace was still fashionable for them, but it became less fashionable after 1850. Many caps were made of alternate bands of ribbon with net or lace. The trimmings were ribbons of different kinds; figured gauze ribbon was often used in the 1840s and 1850s, but heavier ribbons, satin and velvet, were more usual in the 1860s and 1870s. Flowers and sometimes feathers were also added to them. Most of the trimming, knots of ribbon, or flowers and feathers, was placed at the sides over the ears.

Some of the caps gave less covering to the head. Generally, the grander the occasion, the less was worn on the head, but there was also a difference between the headdresses worn by the younger and older women, the married and unmarried. According to fashion journals of the late 1830s, there was then "a mania for covering the head in every costume" (*World of Fashion*, 1838), and this mania apparently continued in the early 1840s. "Caps have not lost anything of their vogue either for morning, dinner or evening dress" (*Ladies' Cabinet*, 1843). Yet the evidence of portraits, and later of photographs, suggests that the head was far less covered by young women at this time than it had been in the 1820s and early 1830s.

An alternative to the cap in 1837 was the turban; but this headdress, which had always been a style for women of mature years, was then just passing out of fashion. Turbans are rare survivors; but as many of them were made of silk and gauze scarves, it is possible that some of the smaller surviving scarves may have been originally made up as turbans. Smaller headdresses of the 1840s were made of narrow gauze and lace scarves. These were arranged in puffs and folds on the head, leaving the forehead and the hair at the back of the head exposed, but usually with ends falling over the ears, or behind them. Small half-handkerchief caps of lace with lappets—the fanchon style— appeared for evening wear in the 1840s. This continued as a cap style until the 1870s, although its aspect changed with the changing hair styles. The fanchon caps of the 1840s and 1850s were usually a single shaped piece of lace or embroidery. The covering of the ears, either with the cap itself, its trimmings or its lappets, is characteristic of the 1840s and 1850s (Fig. 18).

In the late 1850s, when caps had become smaller and were worn increasingly far back on the head, and when younger women were again wearing very little on the head at all, there were three characteristic forms of headdress which were slighter than caps and were linked with the current style of hairdressing. "For a quiet evening party or a concert or a *diner en famille*, the *cachepeigne* of ribbon is in most general demand" (*Ladies' Treasury*, 1859). The *cachepeigne*, which never acquired an English name, was a small crescent of net, stiffened and covered with loops and bands of ribbon. It was set on the hair at the back, sometimes with more loops of ribbon or a fall of lace covering the hair, sometimes with flowers added to it. The second headdress, much worn between 1859 and 1862, was a net of chenille which enclosed the large chignon (Fig. 21). The third headdress, even less of a cap, was a coronet of velvet trimmed with lace, flowers, beads or straw ornament at the front and back, and worn with evening dress in the early 1860s.

In the early 1860s, caps once again became more generally worn and showed the same raised front and the same oval, caul-like shape of the crown as the bonnet. They were usually made of lace or net on a coronet-like frame and had elaborate trimmings of

FIGURE 21.—RATHER A KNOWING THING IN NETS (*Punch, 1860*)
ADMIRING FRIEND.—"Why, Frank! What a capital dodge!"
FRANK.—"A-ya-as. My beard is such a bore, that I have taken a hint from
the fair sex."   (Reproduced by permission of *Punch*.)

lace or ribbon. A cap with oval caul, long from front to back, is
likely to be a cap of the early 1860s. In the later 1860s, as the
chignon rose, caps lost their bag-like effect at the back. Flat leaf-
shapes of net with a rosette at the point, worn in front, lay on the
high hairdressing, and small half-handkerchiefs or diamond
shapes of lace were still worn on the top of the head (Fig. 19).
In the late 1860s, the lappets of these caps were tied either under
the chignon or under the chin. Trimmings of velvet ribbon, edged
with lace on one side, are very characteristic of caps of this time.

The new fashionable cap form of the 1870s was a round soft-
crowned cap worn high on the head. This was particularly a
form for morning caps. The dress caps show a brimless, raised-
crown form, a small version of the hats and bonnets of the late
1870s and early 1880s. They were made of lace, often bead-
trimmed, velvet and crêpe. By 1880, they were usually worn
without lappets or strings. From the mid-1880s to the end of the
century, the wearing of dress caps was more and more limited
to elderly women. Many surviving examples are from this period,
when the dress cap was a fashion limited to age.

CHAPTER 10

GLOVES AND MITTENS

THE length of evening gloves at the opening of Victoria's reign was given clearly in the comment of the *World of Fashion* in June 1837: "Gloves are worn so short in the evening that there is space enough between the trimming which finishes them at the top and the bend of the arm for three or four bracelets". They had been getting shorter for some years. By about 1835, they were half-way between wrist and elbow, and by 1837 covered only a third of this part of the arm. This length remained for evening gloves for the next ten years: "Gloves continue to be worn as they have been for some time past, viz. covering about one-third of the arm and edged with trimmings of lace or ribbon" (*Lady's Newspaper*, 1847).

They were usually of white kid, but pale pink and yellow were also worn. The tops of the gloves were usually trimmed with a ruching of ribbon, but sometimes with lace or flowers. After 1847, the trimmed top ceased to be fashionable, but the practice of wearing several bracelets at the top of the glove continued. During these years, gloves were sometimes ornamented with embroidery on the back of the hand, usually a small spray of flowers in coloured silks or metal thread. They were usually fastened at the wrist with two to four buttons.

The gloves of daytime use were even shorter, just reaching the wrist, fastening with a single button. Buff, yellow or straw-coloured kid was much used for them. A short, single-button kid glove continued for daytime wear during the 1850s and early 1860s. A silk-tasselled braid and clip were sometimes used for fastening instead of a button, and some have a short lacing of silk braid or cord at the back of the wrist, finished with silk tassels as well (Plate 33). The writer of an article on gloves in the *Queen* in 1862, welcoming as a sign of the arrival of spring "the countless pairs of mauve, lemon, pink and my favourite pale-grey", thought these tasselled gloves in bad taste: "Some of the wearers of pink gloves had tassels pendent from their wrists; the pink gloves and the tassels are both in such bad taste that I was glad to see them together". Many of the surviving gloves of this date are in bright blue or green kid as well as in these pale shades. Most of them are finished with a narrow band of white kid at the wrist, but some are pinked in small scallops. A small stud which can be fastened in two positions was used on many of them instead of a button.

Short gloves for evening wear were going out of fashion in 1865, when they lengthened to four, five or six buttons. Evening gloves then continued to get longer, reaching half-way to the elbow during the 1870s, and the elbow and beyond in the early 1880s, fastening with up to twenty buttons from the wrist to the top of the glove. But many of these long gloves of the 1880s show the alternative fastening of a short opening only over the wrist, buttoning with four buttons. From about 1875 to 1890, many gloves were ornamented with lace and embroidery. Kid gloves had embroidery on the backs of the hands in coloured silks or beads. There were also kid gloves frilled with lace at the top, with lace insertions, or with the kid ending just above the wrist, the rest of the glove to the elbow being in a matching, or sometimes contrasting, shade of lace (Plate 36). Grey, cream, tan and black gloves were worn for evening as well as white. ones

The gloves of day wear also grew longer after 1865. Their length from this time until the end of the century varied from a length just covering the wrist, with one or two buttons, to a length more than half-way to the elbow, with eight or ten; but they were never again as short as those of the first half of the reign, which ended only about an inch beyond the lowest part of the thumb. The length varied to fit the length of sleeve, and this was a matter of type of dress as well as date: "When the sleeves are short the gloves must cover the elbow" (*Ladies' Treasury*, 1882). Gloves of four-button length appear to have been the most general during the 1890s.

During the 1860s, gloves were sewn with contrasting silk stitching, such as cerise on grey or black on tan. The earlier stitching on the back of the hand was usually fine and inconspicuous. During the 1860s, it became decoratively obvious. The looped points of the stitching repeat the patterns seen in the applied braids of dress trimmings. During the 1880s and 1890s, the stitching on the backs of the hands was often very heavy. Black gloves with sewings and welts in white, mauve or red were a fashion of the 1890s, and the taste of this decade for the contrast of black and white appeared again in white gloves heavily stitched in black: "White gloves with black strappings continue to be the smartest and these only give place occasionally to the palest shades of dove-grey and tans" (*Lady's Realm*, 1898).

Kid was used for gloves at all times and was always correct and fashionable. White kid gloves were worn for evening dress throughout the century, varying only in length and fastening. Swedish kid, sometimes mentioned in the fashion notes at the beginning of the period, was most highly regarded for its pleasant scent. Throughout the century many of the fashionable gloves worn in England were imported from France or made in England from French skins. The skins of many different animals were used for producing the skin known as kid in the finished glove.

Suède gloves appeared in the 1860s and had become very fashionable by 1880; but in 1882 the fashion received a rebuff; "Her Majesty, having forbidden the *gant de suède* gloves to be worn at the drawing rooms, these are no longer admissible in dress circles" (*Ladies' Treasury*, 1882). By 1890, kid was once again the more fashionable for day and evening wear. Gloves of silk and cotton, machine-knitted in plain or openwork fabric, were worn throughout the period, mostly in informal, country or unfashionable wear. The silk gloves of the 1880s were in what was beginning to be called silk jersey. Like the kid gloves of this date, they were ornamented with insertions, frills and tops of lace, and with embroidery; or plain silk fabric was ruched up the arm. In 1880, gloves of spotted silk matching the fashionable spotted silk dresses were worn. Silk gloves continued to be worn until the end of the century, but were less fashionable by 1890: "Silk gloves have long ceased to be fashionable though thousands of women wear them" (*Woman's World*, 1888).

Woollen gloves, knitted by hand or machine, were not fashionably worn, but the *Englishwoman's Domestic Magazine* in 1861 recommended "for ordinary use" gloves of "cashmere very supple and fitting well".

For riding and travelling a gauntlet style of glove was worn from the beginning to the end of the period (Plate 20). In 1862 the *Queen* illustrated gloves with a fluted border of kid round the wrist "as protection and ornament . . . to supersede the old-fashioned gauntlet", but the gauntlet style remained in gloves for riding, driving and country wear. These were sometimes fur-lined and, at the end of the century, often wool-lined, with a gathering at the wrist for warmth.

Mittens, which are often regarded as a characteristically Victorian accessory, were fashionable for a limited period only. They had become fashionable, for both day and evening wear, in the early 1830s, and continued to be worn during the 1840s. They were of black or white silk, many hand-netted in a simple openwork mesh, worn plain or with the backs lightly embroidered, in silk of the same colour (Fig. 22). Others were made in machine-knitted openwork fabric, giving the effect of a close heavy net. These, too, were plain or embroidered. They were worn short, wrist-length, or long, half-way to the elbow. Long ones could be worn with evening dress and short ones with day dress. The most interesting mittens of this early period are those, usually of black silk, which are embroidered on the backs in a small encrusted pattern in coloured silks, chenille and gold and silver threads, giving the effect of a jewel (Plate 35). These were fashionable in the late 1830s and early 1840s. Later in the 1840s, mittens were netted, crocheted or knitted, like the purses of the time, with gilt or steel beads.

Mittens were not fashionable during the 1850s and 1860s, but were no doubt still worn; some of the very plain examples which survive and are difficult to date may be unfashionable wear of this period. They appear in fashion again, though not very prominently, in the late 1870s and during the 1880s. "Long mittens are worn with demi-toilettes for dinner, but not for dancing parties. They are made in black and in colours to match the dress" (*Queen*, 1879). They were sometimes worn with wedding dress at this time, in white or cream silk. They were in machine-knitted openwork patterns of fine silk, like the openwork of silk stockings of the time; usually they were made in formal meshed patterns, but some were worked with a floral design in the

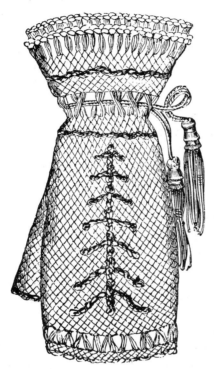

FIGURE 22.—NETTED MITTENS (*Ladies' Companion, 1850*)
Netted in black netting silk darned in colours or in cotton darned in blue wool.

knitting. Mittens were not fashionable during the 1890s; but in 1900, and the early years of the twentieth century, lace mittens, sometimes of hand-made lace, became fashionable, and silk open-work mittens, like those of the 1880s, were again worn.

CHAPTER 11

APRONS

WHEN the reign opened it was fashionable to wear a silk apron as a decorative addition to indoor dress. Aprons of this fashion, which continued to the early 1850s, were often very rich in fabric and ornament: "Aprons are often of richer materials than the dresses with which they are worn" (*Ladies' Companion,* 1851). They were usually long, between twenty-five and thirty inches and were made from two widths of silk, one at the centre and a half at each side, giving a total width of about thirty-five inches. The top was pleated or gathered up into a width of about nine inches, either held in a wide waistband, or in three or four drawings with an attached tasselled cord. The lower edge of the band, in the 1840s, was often shaped to a point to follow the line of the dresses. The aprons often had pockets, some set obliquely into the apron, others applied and ornamented. The usual material was satin, particularly the rich, dark satins, black, blue or green, and, like many other garments and accessories of this time, they had brightly coloured embroidery in silks or chenille against the dark ground (Fig. 23); or they might be trimmed with black silk bobbin lace, or fringe. Printed silks and satins were used. Light coloured satins and silks, striped, checked and shot, might be trimmed with silk braid or fringe. There were also aprons made of velvet and fine woollen fabrics. These, too, might be printed or embroidered, and trimmed with braid or fringe. White muslin aprons in the same form with trimmings of braid, folded vandyke borders and white embroidery, were also worn at this time. Aprons of white muslin were never completely out of fashion at any time. Their date is given by their shape, and by the character and quality of their ornament.

The next group of aprons are those which became fashionable in the early 1860s. These are much smaller than the earlier fashion, about twenty inches long or less, and rounded at the corners. The *Queen*, in 1866, suggested the reason for their revival: "since skirts are gored so that there remains no material to pleat round the waist and in consequence of this style have been found unbecoming to even the slightest figures, aprons have become very favourite additions to both morning and afternoon dresses". Before 1866, these aprons were pleated with flat pleats into narrow pointed waistbands and fastened with cords, plain or tasselled. There was often a button on one end of the cord and a loop on the other for fastening, or buttons at the top corners of the

FIGURE 23.—EMBROIDERED APRON (*Lady's Newspaper, 1849*)
Black satin, embroidered in crimson, blue, green and white silks with cord and tassels.

apron to loop the cord. Black silk was still much used for them, but satin was now far less fashionable than watered silk or grosgrain. Black was the fashion for winter, and coloured silk, matching the trimmings of a white muslin dress, was fashionable for summer. There was a great variety of trimming, velvet ribbon, jet beads, braid and jet beads, embroidery and jet beads, and edging and application of lace, both black and white. The pockets were often outlined with the same trimmings. After 1866, aprons got a little longer and lost the rounded corners and were "no longer cut straight and pleated at the waist, as formerly" (*Queen*, 1868). Now they were gored, so that they would lie flatter against the front of the skirt, which was itself cut in this way. Pleated frills on these aprons suggest a date in the 1870s, but the apron was less in fashion then than in the 1860s.

It had its next period of fashion in the 1880s, but with a slightly less decorative, more utilitarian bias. The fashionable apron of the 1880s was the "bazaar" apron, because "At the numberless bazaars which have recently been held aprons have come into view as a necessary of the ladies acting as stall-keepers" (*Ladies' Treasury*, 1888). Aprons were also worn for playing tennis. For the more workmanlike aprons, canvas with embroidery was often used. Otherwise they were made of almost any material—embroidered muslin, printed cotton, printed or embroidered nun's veiling—but silk was much less used than before. Lace trimming, now nearly always machine-made lace, was very general. An apron with a bib was the usual form of the 1880s, and the bibs by their shaping often reveal the date of the apron. Some were gathered, like the plastrons of the dresses of the 1880s, a detail characteristic of the decade. Others, from the 1890s, have a bib with shoulder-straps and epaulettes to go with the full, leg-of-mutton sleeves. Most aprons of this period have a more flimsy, temporary quality than those of the earlier fashions.

CHAPTER 12

STOCKINGS

PLAIN white stockings were the most usual wear at the beginning of the reign. "On ordinary occasions white stockings harmonize best with the character of the dress, unless it be black, when of course black stockings will be worn" (*Art of Dress*, Anon. 1839). They vary in fabric from the finest of machine-knitted silk to heavier silk, and cotton. If they were in silk, the length of the silk up the leg varied. In many stockings it ends in a cotton top well below the knee, although stockings of the finest quality were silk throughout. Some were quite plain, except for a simple silk clock; others still emphasized the gusset of the heel by a triangle of openwork and embroidery extending over the ankle, and some were patterned in openwork and embroidery over the instep as well. At the time when gloves had frilled tops, some stockings also had a frill of ribbon at the top, an interesting penetration of a current decorative device to a place where it was generally invisible. Stockings of palest mauve or pink silk were worn as well as white ones.

A new type of stocking appeared in the 1860s, worn with the looped-up skirts, which revealed the petticoat beneath. The petticoats were in bright colours, scarlet or magenta, or striped in these colours with white or black. The stockings were in these bright colours, or striped, too. Some were plain white or cream cotton, with clocks in bright red or blue silk. These were the stockings of informal wear; white silk was still the usual wear for evening, and white silk or cotton for more formal daytime wear. Mercerized cotton stockings appeared in the 1850s.

In the 1870s, coloured stockings were worn: "silk or thread coloured stocking is now perfectly admitted by ladies of the greatest elegance and is even considered more fashionable than white" (*Englishwoman's Domestic Magazine*, 1870). For evening wear, black silk would be worn with a black dress and the coloured silk stocking would match the colour of the dress. Stockings of the 1870s and 1880s were often embroidered on the instep and up the front of the leg. The embroidery was either in the same shade as the stocking, or contrasting colour or colours on a neutral ground; it was usually in silk, sometimes in beads. The patterns were usually less formalized than the ornament of the earlier stockings and less limited to the foot and ankle; a single spray of flowers embroidered up the front of the stocking is characteristic of this later ornament. Openwork stockings were also much worn; these were less varied in pattern than earlier examples, but sometimes were made more elaborate with embroidery. A fashion for daytime wear was the stocking in ribbed knitting, sometimes ribbed in contrasting colours.

Black stockings became almost universal for daytime wear in the 1890s; and black was also worn in the evening, except with full evening dress, which still demanded white. Silk stockings were the most fashionable. These were plain for daytime wear, but were made with openwork panels for evening (Plate 30). "Nothing is so becoming to the ankle, so ladylike or so smart, as an openworked black silk stocking or one quite plain with the ever-pretty clockings" (*Lady's Realm*, 1898).

CHAPTER 13

SHOES AND BOOTS

ONE type of Victorian shoe survives in greater numbers than any other, a slim, heelless shoe in black or white satin, which was the fashionable dress shoe from about 1830 to 1860.

This plain, heelless form, which at first sight seems monotonously the same, did change a little within its period of fashion. The pre-Victorian shoe of the 1820s was rounded at the toe. By about 1830, the toe was more nearly square and, by 1840, the shoe had lengthened and narrowed, so that the front was shaped to an almost perfect rectangle, with the sides of the foot showing the minimum of curve (Plate 27). By 1860, although the foot was still square, it was less sharply so and there was some broadening of the foot. The shoes of this early period rarely show any difference for left and right foot.

The usual material for evening dress shoes was white satin and, for formal day dress, black satin. Leather was used for ordinary wear and cloth was also used, sometimes in neutral shades of grey or fawn. The dominance of black and white was broken by a temporary revival of coloured shoes for evening wear in the late 1840s. There are shoes in figured satin from this time and shoes with embroidered fronts. Slippers were made in Berlin woolwork.

Change came in the 1850s when heels began to appear: "somewhat high-heeled shoes are becoming general, not only for walking, but for the ballroom" (*Ladies' Cabinet*, 1850). The height of the heel at this time was an inch or less. The heelless fashion still continued for evening shoes for some years longer, but in the 1860s heels to shoes became general.

A new fashionable attention to shoes and boots completed the change in the 1860s. "A great revolution has taken place in the chaussure of ladies, which generally speaking admits of but little variety. For the black shoe and boot which used to be worn on

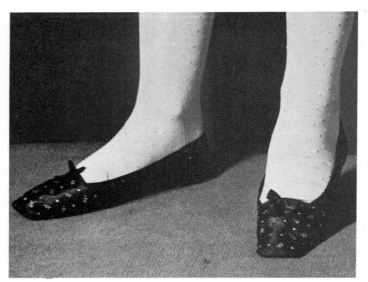

27. Satin shoes, 1835–50
The dark blue satin is figured in white. They show the sharply square toe and long narrow shape which was general for the first half of the reign.

28. Satin wedding boots, 1865
The dress boots of white satin which were worn by a bride in 1865. They have the low heel general in the 1860s and show the continuance of side lacing as an alternative to the elastic gusset.

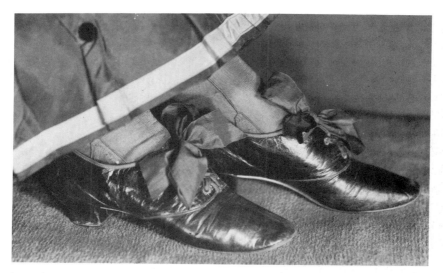

29. Leather shoes, 1875–85

These are walking shoes of brown kid. Shoes with lacing over the instep became fashionable as walking shoes in the 1870s and developed as the usual style for walking during the rest of the century.

30. Leather shoes, 1890–1900

These are dress shoes of black kid with cut-out pattern over a background of red silk and studding of steel beads. They show the pointed toe which, absent for nearly a century, returned to fashion in the 1890s. The stockings are black openwork silk, a general fashion of this time.

nearly all occasions, coloured ones are substituted, to accord nicely with the dress with which they are worn" (*Englishwoman's Domestic Magazine*, 1862). The earlier shoes were very plain, bound round the top with a narrow ribbon, finished at the front with a small, flat bow; often there were long narrow ribbons which crossed over the instep and went round the ankle. In the 1860s the small bow at the front grew to a large bow or rosette, often with a small steel buckle in the centre. Many of the leather shoes of this time had ornamental stitching in contrasting colours and were bound with contrasting ribbon, brown and white on bronze, blue and white, cerise and white on black. Bronze kid was fashionable particularly for indoor shoes from this period to the end of the century.

Boots, like the shoes, were in black and white satin for dress wear, and also in white kid. For walking they were usually in cloth, often grey or fawn, with the toe-caps of matching or black leather. They were ankle-length, and laced up the sides on the inside of the foot. The elastic-side boot, that is, a boot with an elastic gusset at each side, was patented by the firm of Sparkes Hall in 1837 and continued in fashionable wear until about 1870. Satin boots were very generally worn for dress occasions and many surviving examples were worn as wedding boots (Plate 28). The boots showed earlier than the shoes the distinctive shaping for left and right foot, and they acquired heels a little earlier than the shoes. Heels for boots were general by the early 1860s. In the late 1860s, boots with front lacing and boots which buttoned at the sides appeared. Between 1864 and 1868, there was a fashion of ornamenting the top of the boot with tassels. Boots, like shoes, were often made in brightly coloured materials during the 1860s; blue satin was particularly popular.

During the 1870s, the heel, on shoes and boots alike, grew a little higher, became more tapering and was set well under the foot (Fig. 24). Known as the "Louis" heel from the resemblance to the heels of French shoes of the eighteenth century, this form is found on boots and shoes to the end of the period. The height of the heel is usually between one and a half to two inches. The square shaping of the toe gradually changed during the 1870s to a more pointed form; by the mid-1880s, the pointed toe was

FIGURE 24.—SHOES AND BOOTS (*Milliner and Dressmaker, 1874*)

an established fashion, and this style continued, with some lengthening, during the 1890s (Plate 30).

Large rosettes of ribbon gathered into a buckle ornamented the dress shoes of the 1870s; but during the 1880s the large ribbon ornaments disappeared. Shoes with two or three bars across the instep began to appear in the 1870s, and this style, together with a similar style which had a trellis of bars over the instep, was fashionable during the 1880s and continued during the 1890s. Bead embroidery ornamented many shoes of this period and cut-out decoration over a contrasting colour in kid or satin also appeared on shoes of the 1890s (Plate 30). But, by 1890, once more the most fashionable shoes of all were plain and untrimmed, except for a small steel or paste buckle at the centre front. Evening shoes were of white or coloured satin to match the dress.

In the late 1890s, a style appeared with a high shaped front above a large square buckle, which bore some resemblance to the eighteenth-century shoe. Unlike their eighteenth-century prototypes, however, the buckles of these shoes were without prongs and were ornamental, not functional.

A shoe laced over the instep, for walking, appeared in the 1870s and this became the general style for walking shoes during the 1880s and 1890s. The early examples in this style dating from the 1870s and 1880s are usually in soft bronze, black or fawn kid (Plate 29); those of the 1890s are usually black with a toe-cap emphasizing the sharply pointed toe. Black shoes and boots were general for outdoor wear in the 1890s, although fawn was accepted for country wear, and white shoes were worn with white summer dresses.

A few dress boots in white satin or velvet were still worn in the 1870s. Some, like the shoes, had bar fastenings, but in the second half of the period boots were worn mainly for walking or travelling. They were usually in cloth, with a leather galosh, or in leather, laced at the front or buttoned at the side (Fig. 24). During the 1880s and 1890s, they gradually extended higher up the leg, and at the end of the century they had fastenings of about sixteen buttons or pairs of holes for lacing.

CHAPTER 14

BAGS AND PURSES

AT the beginning of the nineteenth century, reticules—or ridicules, as bags were then called—were fashionable, because the new slim skirts of muslin would have been disfigured if pockets of eighteenth-century style had been worn beneath them: and they continued in use in spite of the return of the wider skirt in the 1830s.

Many of the bags of the first few years of the Victorian period were made to match the dress or bonnet, and were often worn hanging from the belt. The most attractive Victorian bags come from these years. *The Workwoman's Guide,* published in 1838, says: "Bags are made of silk, satin, velvet and many other materials and are almost always lined. . . . There is a great variety of shapes and they are trimmed with fringe, lace, ribbon, silk, &c, &c." The great variety of shapes included flat bags, square with the top frilled above a drawstring, or spade-shaped; and full, round bags with frilled, or stiffened, tops. They fastened with a drawstring of ribbon or cord, a flap or a metal clasp. The metal clasps of this period were often very decorative, being silver gilt or pinchbeck in scrolled and floral designs (Plate 32). The actual fastening mechanism was usually a stud which was pressed to open them. The bag of 1839—illustrated in Plate 31—shows another characteristic shape of this date; characteristic, too, is its edging of blonde lace. Seams of bags, like the seams of dresses, were at this time often piped, and piping is good evidence for a date between 1830 and 1850.

The bags of the 1830s shared the predilection of that decade for bright colours against a dark ground, and a great many of them were made of dark blue or black satin decorated with bright embroidery. The ornament of this time may be appliqué of narrow silk ribbon (Plate 31), appliqué of puffed and padded crêpe or embroidery in chenille thread, as well as embroidery in silk stitchwork. A combination of all these techniques may appear in one bag. Bags of fine seed-like beads, closely netted into elaborate patterns resembling the bead purses of the late seventeenth century, were made in the 1830s and 1840s (Plate 32); and black and dark blue velvet bags, embroidered with steel or gilt beads, were a fashion of the 1840s.

Bags embroidered in coloured silks in cross- or tent-stitch on fine canvas are likely to come from the 1830s or 1840s. These often had a central spray of flowers within a floral border, and the canvas background between was left unstitched. By 1850, wool embroidery in bright colours—Berlin woolwork—was much practised, and bags were amongst the many objects worked in this technique during the 1850s and 1860s.

To some extent the use of bags increased or decreased according to the size and nature of the skirt. The late 1840s probably produced fewer bags than the 1830s and early 1840s, for pockets are more often found in dresses of 1845 to 1855 than in dresses of the first years of the reign. Skirts grew even larger in the late 1850s and 1860s, but their fullness was spread more smoothly over the crinoline and once again there was a greater use of bags, particularly with thin muslin dresses. Bags were once more worn hanging from the waistband and were then called chatelaine bags. "For some time past chatelaine bags have been very popular in England. They have been worn at the side suspended to the waistband. These have generally been made of leather and studded with steel, and for travelling have been found very convenient. For home wear they are made of gimp or embroidered velvet" (Queen, 1863). Judging from surviving examples the most popular shape at this time seems to have been a flat bag, about six inches square, in Berlin woolwork; this was lined with silk or satin and outlined with silk cord, usually with tassels at the top corners and a silk cord for carrying or hanging from the waist (Plate 32). Another style, illustrated in the Queen in 1868 was shaped to three points, each with a tassel. This was called a card purse, for one of the uses of bags was to hold the slim case of ivory, tortoiseshell or mother-of-pearl, which held the visiting cards. This example was of cashmere, embroidered with silk and cord. The use of cashmere in a bag, especially if its ornament is

31. Bags, 1835–50
(top, right) *Purple satin embroidered in small beads of white and clear glass.*
(top, left) *Black satin embroidered with coloured silks, narrow shaded ribbon and chenille.*
(below right) *Cream silk, edged with silk bobbin lace, preserved with a wedding dress of 1839.*

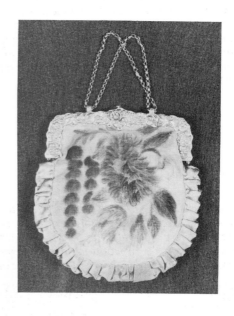

32. Bags, 1835–70

(above left) *Small, coloured glass beads closely netted on a foundation of fine cotton, 1835–60.*

(above right) *Cream velvet painted in various colours and edged with pleated blue satin; gilt metal frame embossed with a design of flowers. Painting on velvet was a popular accomplishment of the 1840s and 1850s.*

(right) *Canvas embroidered with wool in cross stitch* Berlin woolwork *in various colours against a purple ground. Cord and tassels are of yellow silk, the cord threaded through small rings at the top of the bag, 1850–70.*

33. Purses and gloves, 1835–65

(right) *Purse of pink silk knitted with small steel beads in upper half and white silk knitted with looped fringes of clear glass and steel beads in lower half; set in steel frame with stud fastening. Purses of this kind were called 'shaggy bead' purses (Ladies Knitting and Netting Book, 1839).*

(below) *Purse of pink silk and metal thread netted with steel beads, steel bead tassel at one end, steel bead fringe at the other, and steel rings. The short white kid gloves which fasten with one button have the back lacing with tasselled cord often seen in gloves of the early 1860s.*

34. Bags and purse, 1880–1900

(above right) *Bag of green-blue plush, metal frame with sliding catch; with matching purse which has a knobbed fastening very general in the last quarter of the century and continuing in use in the twentieth century, 1880–90.*

(above left) *Bag of black leather with metal frame fastening in the same way as the plush bag, 1890–1900.*

(left) *Detail of the slide fastening on the leather bag.*

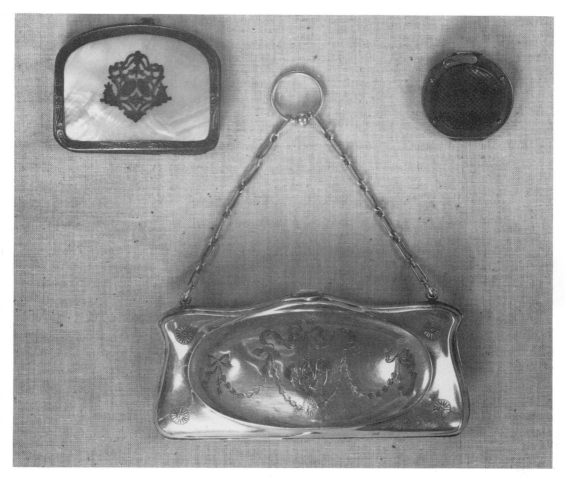

Purses, 1860–1900
(above left) *Purse mother-of-pearl on leather with applied silver ornament on one side, 1860–75.*

(above)   *Silver purse 1898–9. The finger ring on the chain is a particular characteristic of purses of the 1890's.*

(above right and below right)   *Sovereign purse of leather on metal frame (diam. 3.75 cm).*

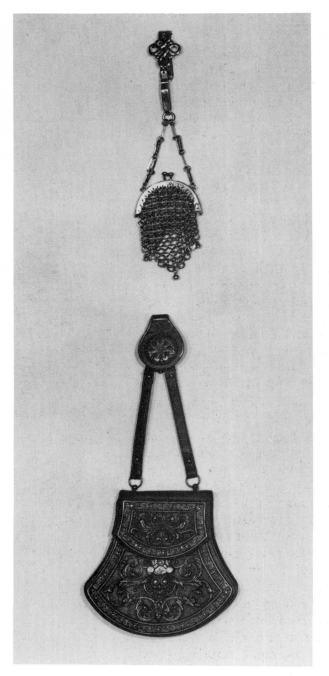

34. Chatelaine purse and bag, 1870–1900

Purse of steel mesh and frame with steel hook for hanging from waistband or belt, 1890–1900.

Bag of black leather with applied ornament of embossed metal with hook for hanging from waistband or belt, 1870–80.

appliqué or braid embroidery, suggests a date in the late 1860s
or 1870s. A type of embroidery which flourished particularly
between 1865 and 1870 was embroidery on bed ticking: this
appeared on bags, usually on the flat wallet-shaped type. Bags
were also made in crochet with silk thread, particularly during
the 1840s and 1850. These were round in shape, with a tassel at
the bottom and a drawstring at the top. Bags of this kind which
have a kid lining were made as tobacco pouches for men.

In the 1870s, rather large bags of black velvet on a heavy silver
clasp with hook or clip attached, were worn as chatelaine bags.
The clasps and their ornament were much heavier than the
delicately ornamented clasps on the bags of the beginning of the
period. Chatelaine bags continued to be worn from the waist with
the slimmer skirts of the late 1870s (Plate 34) and early 1880s.
"Pockets in skirts are still impossible for if they contain anything
beyond the finest of handkerchiefs they bulge and make themselves ungracefully apparent. The result is that chatelaine bags
are adopted by those who may require to carry card-case and
purse, besides the necessary handkerchief, for as the spring wears
on the convenient muff-bags must be dispensed with" (*Queen*,
1882). The chatelaine bags were now of velvet, satin or plush,
a favourite material of the 1880s. The muff-bags, which were
mainly a fashion of the 1880s, were either a bag serving as a muff,
or a muff with a bag attached, usually in fur, velvet or plush. In
the late 1880s bags were still worn, but by then they were usually
called dress bags. By 1880, the term handbag was being used to
distinguish a bag which was carried from one which was worn.

The silk and velvet bags of the 1880s and 1890s are simple in
construction, often just a rectangle of material folded in two, the
sides sewn together, and frilled with a drawstring. Some are
embroidered and some lace-trimmed as well, but the lace is now
usually machine-made. The *Ladies' Treasury* suggested "for carrying prayer and hymnbook", in 1894, a bag of violet velvet,
embroidered in gold spots, lined with cream satin and frilled at
top and bottom with cream lace. Embroidery on bags of this time
is usually more sparse and economical of stitchery than that of
the earlier bags and is in looser, more naturalistic floral designs,
or freely adapted formal motifs. "Beetle-wing" embroidery, an

appliqué of iridescent green spangles—a fashion of the late 1880s and 1890s—is found ornamenting bags of this date; and on bags of the 1890s embroidery in ribbon appears once again, a revival of work popular in the 1830s.

Up to this time the leather handbag on a metal frame was less common than bags of other kinds, but during the 1880s it began to appear more frequently. From this date onwards bags bear a general resemblance to bags of the present time (Plate 34). The leather handbags of the 1890s were often made of morocco leather, green being a favourite colour, mounted on a silver or other metal frame, and lined with silk. They might have elaborate fittings or they might have no fittings at all. In one issue of the *Queen*, in June 1897, there were advertisements for three types of leather handbag, each with a different name: "a visiting bag" was fitted with purse, card-case and scent-bottle; "an opera bag" was described as "completely fitted", and its fittings included opera glasses and powder-puff, an accessory just beginning to be accepted; but "a shopping or visiting bag" of green or maroon morocco was "quite empty". In another issue of the same year "a matinée bag" was advertised; it was fitted with scent bottle, opera glasses and biscuit case.

The Victorians used purses of various kinds, but one above all is characteristic. This is a narrow tube of silk, eight to ten inches long, netted, knitted or crocheted, with or without the addition of beads, with tasselled ends and a short slit in the length at the centre closed by two rings—or slides to give them their contemporary name—usually of metal. These purses have since been called stocking purses, miser's purses, or ring-purses; but in their own time they were simply purses until the 1860s, when they were beginning to pass out of fashion; then, to distinguish them from other shapes, they were called long purses.

The long purse is not an exclusively Victorian form. It was the purse of the eighteenth century and the early nineteenth century, and so at the beginning of the reign of Victoria it already had a long history. The eighteenth-century purses were mostly on a larger scale than those of the nineteenth century. They were usually handknitted in silk, their ornament being the pattern of the knitting, but sometimes in more decorative examples, metal thread was worked with the silk. They might be with or without tassels at the ends. There seems to have been no distinction between those carried by men and those carried by women. Green was the most usual colour for them, a colour still popular in the early nineteenth century. Becky Sharp, in her apprentice days, tried to ensnare the affections of Joe Sedley with a netted purse of green silk. Thackeray wrote of this in the 1840s, from recollection of a generation earlier, perhaps thinking of Jane Austen's Mr. Bingley, who scarcely knew any young lady who could not paint tables, cover screens and net purses. The simple netted mesh was a square or lozenge shape, with a knot at each corner. The netted purses which Jane Austen knew were about six to eight inches long, smaller than the Victorian purses and far smaller than those of the eighteenth century. Many were of plain, meshed silk; some were worked with beads in the mesh, giving a dew-spangled effect; others were netted more closely with small coloured beads so that only the beads were visible. The tassels were pendent drops—very often in the form of an acorn—in mother-of-pearl, pinchbeck or silver filigree, and the closing rings matched them. The purse of the early nineteenth century shaded gradually into the Victorian purse during the 1830s, but there is a clear difference between the purses made before 1830 and those made after 1840.

The Victorian long purses were made and used from the beginning of the reign until about 1880. Directions for working them, in knitting, netting, and crochet, appeared in journals throughout this period, although less often after 1870. The *Lady's Knitting Book*, published in 1879, gives instructions for making them with the comment: "these old-fashioned long purses are still occasionally used". Within their period, 1840 to 1870, it is not easy to date any example very exactly or to distinguish, for instance, a purse made in 1850 from one made in 1860.

There are two shapes, one with both ends round, with a tassel at each end; the other with one round end with a tassel and one flat end with a fringe of beads or two or three silk tassels (Plate 33). Both shapes were made throughout the period and difference of shape is no sign of date; nor is it any mark of the sex of the user. These purses, like those of the eighteenth century, were carried by men and women—or, at least, many were made for men. Some of the working instructions are for "a gentleman's purse", some for "a lady's purse", but many simply for "a purse" and there seems to be no difference. A gentleman's purse of 1850 was worked in cerise and blue silk, crocheted, with a pattern at the ends in steel and gold beads, and with one end round with a bead tassel and the other flat with a steel bead fringe; but the lady of James Collinson's painting, "The Empty Purse" (1857), carries just such a purse (Plate 3). A lady's purse of 1850 was knitted— on a pair of No. 18 pins—in bright blue and white purse silk, with gold and steel beads and with a tassel of mixed gold and steel beads at each end.

Steel bead ornament is characteristic of the Victorian long purse. The small coloured beads used for the earlier purses were little used after 1850. Gilt beads were used, but steel beads and bugles were the most usual decoration for purses of the 1850s and 1860s. The beads were threaded on to the silk of the purse and worked with it, either all over the surface or in bands of pattern at the ends. The tassels and fringes at the ends were also of steel beads. The rings which close the purses were in faceted steel or gilt, matching the beading.

The thread used in the making of the purses was nearly always silk, and was known as purse silk or netting silk. It was netted, knitted or crocheted. All these techniques were used from the beginning to the end of the period, but netting and knitting seem to have been less used, and crochet more used, after 1850. Tatting, which became popular in the 1850s, was occasionally used but, popular as it was for many other accessories, it was not much used for purse making.

Long purses of fabric, silk, velvet or fine wool, embroidered with silk or beads are found, but they are much less common and usually less attractive than the characteristic form.

Although the long purse was so often made and used, it was not the only form of its time. There are purses, also netted, knitted or crocheted, with or without beads, which are small bags, with a tassel at the bottom and a drawstring at the top. Others, instead of fastening with a drawstring, have a gilt or steel clasp— miniatures of the bags which are their contemporaries (Plate 33).

Some purses are very small and round, about half an inch in diameter, on a curved metal clasp. These are sovereign purses. Similar purses in leather or suède are also found (Plate 34). There are also sovereign purses of metal, some of which are shaped like a watchcase, others like a small cylinder. They are easily recognized from the close relation of their size and shape to the small gold coins they were made to hold. The leather and metal ones are likely to be from the last thirty years of the period and the handworked ones from the first thirty years.

Although there was so much making of purses by amateurs, there are also purses of leather which were the work of professional pursemakers. The leather purses of the first half of the period, plain or silk-lined, are of two or three compartments, mounted on a metal frame enclosed in covers of ivory, tortoiseshell or mother-of-pearl (Plate 34). They are usually rectangular, rounded at the corners, or with a slightly curved top. Purses of plush were fashionable in the 1880s (Plate 34) and fur purses in the 1880s and 1890s. Plain leather purses with a flap fastening were in use in the 1870s. By the 1890s, leather was the usual material for purses, morocco, crocodile or lizard, and they were usually made with a flap fastening or on a metal frame which fastened with a clasp at the top. They often have frames or mounts of silver bearing hall-marks, which are a useful guide to their date. Purses of metal and metal mesh may belong to the 1890s, but are more characteristic of the early years of the twentieth century.

CHAPTER 15

FANS

AT the beginning of the reign the fan was a far less important accessory than it had been in the eighteenth century or even in the first quarter of the nineteenth century. The fans of the early nineteenth century were generally fairly small and plain, with leaves of thin silk spangled and lightly painted; their sticks, also, compared with those of earlier fans, were plain and unornamented. There were also small brisé fans—fans without a leaf—whose sticks, of thin ivory or wood, pierced, carved and linked together with ribbon, extended to form the whole fan. These, also, were sometimes painted, either in small motifs on each stick or with a single motif over the open fan.

Fans in the eighteenth-century style reappeared in the 1840s, fans with sticks of ivory or mother-of-pearl elaborately carved and gilded, with leaves of vellum, each a small-scale, beautifully executed painting. The paintings were copies of those on eighteenth-century fans, or scenes painted *à la Watteau* (Plate 35). These elaborate fans were imported from France into England; but most of the fans used in this country during the period were imported, from France, China or Japan. At the time of the Fan Exhibition at South Kensington in 1870 it was stated that fan-making as a trade was little represented in London where, out of seven or eight firms given in the directory, one only was English, the rest being French. Several French artists worked in this medium and many fan painters and stick ornamenters worked as known artists.

The most costly and aristocratic of nineteenth-century fans were made in this eighteenth-century style, but not all the surviving fans made in this traditional style were of the first quality. The cheaper ones had leaves of painted paper. The treatment of the painted figures and their dress will usually, if compared with an eighteenth-century fan, reveal the nineteenth-century origin.

35. Fan and Mittens, 1835–50

The fan with painted paper leaf and sticks and guards of mother-of-pearl, carved and gilded, is in the eighteenth century style. The mittens of machine-knitted black silk are embroidered in gold and silver thread, green and red silk and beads in the fashion of the late 1830s and early 1840s for dress mittens.

36. Fan and gloves, 1880–90
Fan with black satin leaf embroidered in golden yellow silk, edged with matching lace, wooden sticks and guards and black silk tassel. Gloves of pale brown kid and matching silk in machine-knitted openwork pattern.

A new nineteenth-century leaf may, of course, replace an earlier damaged one, so that a fan may have eighteenth-century sticks and a nineteenth-century leaf.

By the 1860s the fan was more generally fashionable and popular, and there are fans of all kinds from this period. Many of the cheaper fans are attractive and are more essentially of their moment than the costly fans executed in the grand manner. Amongst them are fans of crêpe with spangled decoration, which had reappeared in the 1850s. The 1860s have their characteristic spangles of steel cut in star or flower-shapes, and often fretted (Plate 37). The sticks are often rather broad, in wood, bone or ivory, with coarse geometric piercing and fretted designs, sometimes with a spotted inlay of steel spangles. Fans which have a small oval leaf at the top of each stick are also a style of this decade (Plate 37). Fans of plain or watered silk were painted with wreaths of flowers or with figures. There was a good deal of amateur fan-painting during the second half of the century. The famous firms of Duvelleroy and Rimmel sold plain fans for this purpose of ivory, or of the cheaper, white-enamelled wood. Small brisé fans of sandalwood, which were the fans of outdoor use, were also painted. Flowers and birds were the usual subjects for their decoration (Plate 37); but, according to the *Englishwoman's Domestic Magazine*, a dog's head or one of the favourite race-horses of the time was a popular subject in 1866. The fans of the middle of the century are of small to medium size, usually between six and ten inches in length.

By 1870, the fan was once more universally used: "No toilette can be considered complete without a fan" (*Queen*, 1870). The large number of fans which survive from the 1870s and 1880s is witness of this. Fans of the 1870s usually have broad and heavy sticks with varied shaping. Their leaves are usually silk or satin, and are often lace-trimmed, embroidered or painted. Some of them were trimmed with a light feather-edging, usually of marabout; this edging is, however, also found on fans of the 1860s (Plate 37), and occasionally on those of the 1840s and 1850s.

Feather fans were popular in the 1870s (Plate 38). Feathers of many different kinds appear in fans of this date—cock's, pea-

37.   Fans, 1860–75

(above) *Brisé fan ivory sticks and guards painted with a Chinese design.*

(below) *Sticks and guards of carved ivory with a small silk leaf on each stick ornamented with fretted spangles; feather edging along the top of the leaves, 1860–70.*

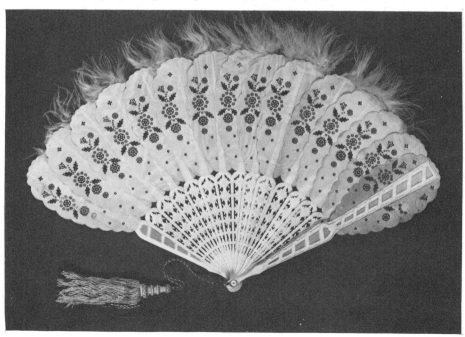

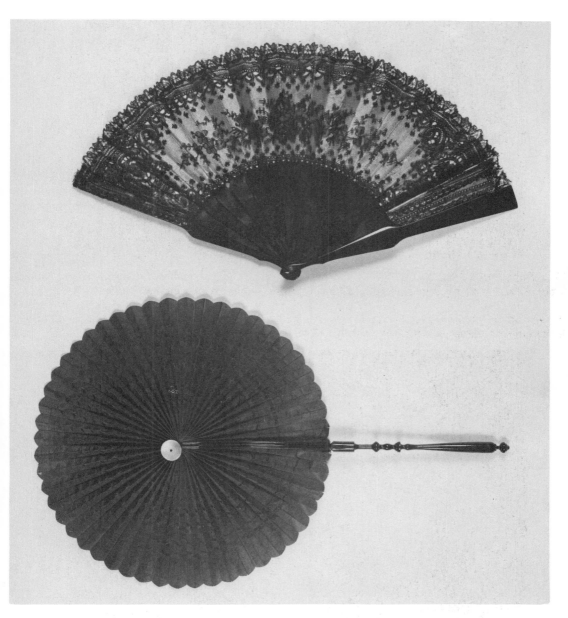

(above) *Leaf of black silk bobbin lace over cream silk, tortoiseshell sticks and guards.*

(below) *Parasol fan of pleated green silk which folds back into the turned wood handle.*

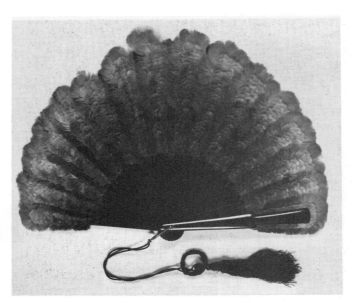

38. Fans, 1870–1900
(left) *Leaf of feathers shading from dark to light grey, sticks and guards black wood with black silk tassel, 1875–85.*

(below) *Leaf of white muslin painted in black and white and edged with black lace, ivory sticks and guards, 1880–1900.*

Brisé fan, ivory with painted decoration 1870–80.

Leaf of silk muslin, spangled and painted, mother-of-pearl sticks and guards. This and the fan above are approximately half the size of the black and white fan shown on the opposite page.

cock's, pheasant's and pigeon's. There are examples of painted quill fans from the 1840s, but fans which make decorative use of contrasting kinds of feathers of different natural shadings and patterns, and of natural and dyed feathers, are likely to be of the 1870s. Feather was also used for fans of the screen type, which had a renewed popularity from the late 1870s to the end of the century; sometimes these are adorned with a small bird, complete and stuffed, a fashionable decoration which is found nestling on many garments and accessories of the 1880s.

The fashion for ostrich fans came in the late 1880s and continued through the 1890s and the early years of the next century: "Leaders of fashion prefer about sixteen magnificent ostrich feathers mounted on tortoiseshell" (*Lady's World*, 1887). Ostrich feather fans were usually black or white, the black being mounted on tortoiseshell sticks and the white on mother-of-pearl sticks; the sticks were usually plain.

Fans with leaves entirely of bobbin or needlepoint lace became fashionable in the 1860s and remained fashionable until the end of the century. At the Paris Exhibition of 1878, lace fans were by far the most numerous amongst the fans exhibited, and fans with leaves of finest needlepoint and bobbin lace rivalled the ceremonial fans of the eighteenth-century tradition in costliness during the last quarter of the century.

Many fans survive with leaves of good quality lace. Fans with leaves of the black silk bobbin lace of Chantilly were particularly fashionable in the 1860s (Plate 37). The looser laces without net ground, Belgian and Honiton bobbin laces, Honiton appliqué on machine net, and the fine needlepoint—*point de gaze*—are more characteristic of the 1880s and 1890s. Many of the fans described as "point lace" fans in the 1870s were worked in a popular technique of this time, in which a ready-made braid was mounted on net or linked with embroidery stitches.

A characteristic style of the 1870s was a revival of the early nineteenth-century parasol fan. This was a silk fan, usually plain, whose pleated leaf spread out into a circle at the top of a handle (Plate 37). A fan of this kind appears also in Collinson's painting of 1857 (Plate 3). In the 1870s, fans were sometimes worn suspended from a cord round the waist, and many of the surviving fans of this time have a short cord and tassel. A bow of ribbon often replaced the cord and tassel in the 1880s.

Fans of the 1880s are distinguished by their very large size, being usually between fourteen and sixteen inches in length (Plates 36 and 38). The sticks are slim and light. The large gauze or satin leaves were painted with naturalistic sprays of flowers or birds and sometimes with figures. The *à la Watteau* influence never left the nineteenth-century fan, but some of the fans of the 1880s were painted with contemporary scenes. Full-blown silk flowers were sometimes added to a painted leaf, or the leaves themselves might be made of layers of silk petals. Black leaves with painted or embroidered decoration in bright or light colours (Plate 36), or with steel spangles, were also in fashion in the 1880s. Fans with a curve more elliptical than circular, with sticks at the side shorter than those at the centre, were a characteristic style of the 1880s and were sometimes referred to as "Fontange fans".

The large fans continued to be used in the early 1890s (Fig. 10), but by the mid-1890s small fans were once again becoming fashionable. They had leaves of muslin, lightly painted and much spangled, and mother-of-pearl sticks (Plate 38). They were usually referred to as "Empire fans" and bore a slight resemblance to the fans of the early years of the nineteenth century which inspired them. "Fans are either very costly painted by a master artist or composed of priceless lace; or they are merely made in the softest gossamer material to match the dress worn at the time and only serve to finish the toilette and make it complete" (*Woman's World*, 1890).

Brisé fans of pierced ivory and wood in Chinese designs were imported from China throughout the century. They varied in size and shape with the prevailing fashion, but were constant also to a European conception of Chinese work (Plate 37). Japanese fans, with slim sticks and painted paper leaves, were amongst the cheaper fans in use at the end of the century.

CHAPTER 16

HANDKERCHIEFS

THE fan was in eclipse in the early 1840s. Instead of a fan, a bouquet or an elaborately ornamented handkerchief was carried in the hand. The ornament of the handkerchief was the delicate white embroidery on muslin which was fashionable during the 1830s and 1840s. Delicacy of white embroidery and its profusion in dress were at this time marks of elegant and expensive costume.

Handkerchiefs of this period are of two kinds. There are the ordinary handkerchiefs of daily use, called morning handkerchiefs in the fashion journals. These may be of muslin or lawn with a hemstitched border, half an inch or an inch broad, and an edging of narrow bobbin lace, Lille, Valenciennes or the English Midlands lace. Sometimes they may have a narrow rolled hem instead of the hemstitched border, and may have three or four lines of openwork within it. Handkerchiefs with printed borders in flower patterns may also be found. These were described at the time as ladies' riding handkerchiefs. There were, also, quite plain handkerchiefs of linen or muslin.

The dress handkerchiefs were much richer, and elaborate with embroidery and lace. At no other time in the reign did the handkerchief have quite so much skill and attention lavished on it as in this first decade. The muslin or lawn is finer than that used for morning handkerchiefs, the borders are richly and deeply worked in white embroidery, and the handkerchief is often edged with lace broader than that of the morning handkerchiefs. The white embroidery, raised satin stitch and openwork on muslin or lawn, was an industry in Scotland. It was often at this time called "Scotch needlework" and later "Ayrshire work" (M. Swain, *The Flowerers*, 1955). The patterns are usually floral, with feathery leaves and sprays (Fig. 25). Some of the dress handkerchiefs have rounded corners, and some have scalloped edges, shaped by the floral pattern, particularly those of the early 1850s. All handkerchiefs of this time are rather large, about twenty-five inches square, but many of them are not exact squares.

These dress handkerchiefs with their fine embroidery are an attractive accessory to collect; they provide a wonderful pattern-book of designs in white embroidery. They also give a collection of lace in a way which shows it to great advantage. It is possible that many dress handkerchiefs which now survive without a lace edging had one originally, for the finer laces are likely to have been removed. From a practical point of view, also, these handkerchiefs have an appeal, as they are easy to mount, store and display, and they take up very little space.

FIGURE 25.—EMBROIDERY FOR HANDKERCHIEFS (*Lady's Newspaper, 1851*)
Worked in cotton in raised satin stitch.

Embroidered, lace-trimmed handkerchiefs survive from every period of the nineteenth century, but the later handkerchiefs never again achieve the quality and interest of those of this first period. The fine raised satin stitch embroidery on muslin was still worked on handkerchiefs after openwork embroidery, now known as *broderie anglaise*, became fashionable again in the 1850s and took its place on other accessories. But the later embroidery has lost its first freshness; its designs are stiffer and more repetitive. During the 1850s, the embroidering of the whole border diminished to the embroidering of the corners. The embroidered corner may include initials, the initials themselves being elaborated into designs. Many alphabets for embroidery appear in the journals of the 1850s and 1860s, and elaborately embroidered initials or full names are found on many handkerchiefs. Other ornaments had brief periods of fashion. A writer in the *Queen* in 1865 remarked that "Bees and butterflies have adorned our pocket-handkerchiefs, our collars and sleeves for many months, and these winged insects are to be superseded by swallows, embroidered in satin stitch"; but the butterfly still appeared in designs for handkerchiefs in the same journal five years later. The monogram appears sometimes in the centre of the handkerchief, not in a corner (*Queen*, 1879). During the 1860s, embroidery and lace edging were often added to handkerchiefs woven with striped borders. Embroidery grew less elaborate during the second half of the period. Now only one corner was embroidered with a simple design, or initials no longer so large or elaborate as those of the middle years of the century. A scalloped edging enclosing a border of embroidered dots was also a handkerchief style of the late nineteenth century.

The use of coloured cotton for the embroidery of handkerchiefs appears in examples from the 1850s onwards. In the 1860s, it was the custom to have morning handkerchiefs with coloured borders, or a scalloped edge or corner embroidered in coloured cotton to match a dress or its trimmings. This fashion continued through the 1870s and 1880s.

Coloured cambric handkerchiefs, in pale colours, appeared in the last few years of the century.

Evening handkerchiefs were still trimmed with all varieties of bobbin and needlepoint lace, particularly Valenciennes, which remained the favourite edging and insertion lace for handkerchiefs during the second half of the period. "Nothing is more ladylike than a good cambric handkerchief with a tolerably wide hem edged with narrow Valenciennes lace" (*Queen*, 1898). During the 1860s, muslin appliqué on net also appeared as a handkerchief border; and borders were also worked in crochet, tatting and the so-called "point-lace" (see page 170). The corners of handkerchiefs of this time may be, like the earlier ones, rounded, and sometimes the bordering lace or net appliqué was shaped into the muslin. Lace insertion instead of, or as well as, lace edging appeared in handkerchiefs from the 1860s to the end of the century. Handkerchiefs of the 1860s and 1870s were smaller than the earlier ones, being about eighteen inches square. The handkerchief, particularly the dress or ornamental handkerchief, grew smaller throughout the century and at the end was sometimes no more than a small circle of silk, lawn or muslin within a deep border of lace, making a square of about twelve inches.

CHAPTER 17

MUFFS

MUFFS were carried during the winter months for most of the reign, although the fashion never at any time appears to have been universal. The muff had periods of greater or less popularity and there is one important change of style which came in the late 1870s. There is some variation in size and shape; but the very large muff falls outside the period, as it was fashionable in the early years of the century and was just coming into fashion again at the end.

In the first half of the reign the muff was usually a fur one. The kind of fur varies, partly according to the changing fashion in furs and partly according to the means of the wearer. Muffs of ermine were particularly fashionable from the beginning of the reign until about 1860, when they began to appear more rarely in the costume of fashionable women but were still regarded as suitable for children's wear. Sable and chinchilla were also popular during the 1840s and 1850s. Muffs of this date were of medium size, a firm padded cylinder in form, about nine inches long with a circumference of about twenty inches. They were lined with silk, often quilted. The lining was drawn up at the ends by a ribbon tied in a bow. There were also velvet and satin muffs of the same shape, with a fur or swansdown border round each end.

A fashion note in the *World of Fashion* for 1845 said that muffs were made of every kind of fur, "with their usual accompaniment, these useful manchettes". These fur cuffs, which are sometimes found making a set with a muff, were a fashion of the 1840s, although they also received fashionable mention again in the 1880s.

During the late 1850s, muffs became smaller and remained small for the next twenty years: "we are accustomed in England to see small muffs—if they are barely large enough to admit the two hands their dimensions are considered quite sufficient"

(*Queen*, 1863). Sable was the first fur of the 1860s, chinchilla was still used and astrakhan became fashionable at this time. Sable remained the most prized of all furs until the end of the century. Muffs of grebe feathers were also a fashion of the middle years of the century. Fabric muffs, particularly velvet ones bordered with fur, continued to be used in the 1860s and 1870s. Like the fur muffs, they were usually smaller than the similar muffs from the early part of the reign.

Skunk was a fur of the 1870s, and astrakhan remained fashionable, but chinchilla was less used until the last years of the century, when it once more became fashionable. The fur muffs of the 1870s were often drawn up each end with a tasselled cord, an ornament which continued until the late 1880s. A muff of cock's feathers was described in the *Queen* as the newest muff for the season of 1876. Up to the end of the 1870s, muffs were either a simple cylinder of fur or a similar shape in fabric with bands of fur bordering the ends. From about 1879 to 1890, the muff appeared in new shapes and new mixtures of material. Muffs of satin, plush and velvet, trimmed with lace appeared in 1879. During the 1880s, these plush and satin muffs, ornamented with fur, lace and ribbon, were as popular as fur muffs. They no longer followed the usual, simple muff form, but were elaborate in shaping and decoration. They were often loose and bag-shaped, and many of them were muff and bag combined. A characteristic ornament was a large bow of ribbon placed centrally, or at one side, and sometimes a small stuffed bird, a favourite ornament everywhere at this time, rested on them. The bows and birds also ornamented the fur muffs of the 1880s, for which astrakhan, fox, stone-marten, beaver and seal were popular furs.

In the 1890s, the muff returned to its plainer traditional form. Some were still small, but the fashion for larger, rather flat muffs became the dominant one, and the size at the end of the century was medium to large. Sable was still the favourite fur, but mink, chinchilla, astrakhan and fox were all used. The fashion for having the head and tail of the animal on the muff appeared in the 1890s.

CHAPTER 18

PARASOLS

PARASOLS to protect the face from the sun are a dress accessory now almost extinct, for today women turn their bare heads and faces to the sun like worshippers. When Queen Victoria came to the throne, the face was encircled by the brim of the bonnet, veiled at will with a bonnet veil and, as a third line of defence, shaded beneath a parasol.

The parasols of the reign fall into three groups. The small parasols, with slender and usually folding sticks, are of the early Victorian period, from the beginning of the reign until about 1865. After 1865, parasols take on a heavier look with thicker handles and more solid ferrules, and they increase in size and sturdiness in the late 1870s and 1880s. Then in the last decade of the reign and century the parasol blossoms again with new, larger elegance. Large and long-handled, it develops after 1896 a new characteristic, a rich elaboration of the lining.

The fashion for small parasols opens almost exactly with the reign. The fashionable parasols of its first summer were "Victoria parasols for open carriages". They were "perfectly calculated for that purpose of a very small size and with folding sticks so that they may be used to shade the face as a fan, they are composed of *poult de soie chinée*. Some are trimmed with fringes, others have an embroidered border—all are pretty. As to the sticks, they are of wrought ivory and of antique patterns" (*World of Fashion*, 1838). This gives the general style of parasol for the first period. It stands in sharp contrast with the parasols of the 1820s and the early 1830s, which were larger and heavier, and had covers almost always of a single colour, usually green or brown, in plain twilled silk. In the late 1830s, handles and ferrules became slimmer and the parasol itself smaller. The difference between the parasols of the 1840s and the parasols which were used earlier in the century is thus clearly marked. There was no general change of style again until the 1860s, although there was much variety of detail.

Within this first period of the reign the parasols show variety not only according to their date, but also according to their use and quality. Up to this time the parasol had not been a part of dress on which great expenditure had been lavished, and the utilitarian element was predominant in even the most elegant of the early nineteenth-century examples; but the carriage parasol of the 1840s was an object of elegant display. The walking parasols were plainer, sometimes without a fringe, and they had a long stick ferrule (Plate 19) instead of the small knob or ring of the carriage parasol. A pointed ferrule of carved ivory, a small version of the ferrule of the 1820s, is a link with the earlier parasols and is a sign of a date at the opening of the period (Plate 39).

The most elegant carriage parasols have handles of ivory, coral or mother-of-pearl, worked in elaborate designs, beautifully cut. These elaborate handles are particularly characteristic of the 1840s, but they are found only in the more expensive parasols, and many handles of the simpler, but still gay and attractive parasols are plainly turned in ivory or wood. The stick to which the handle was attached was usually of wood, but some parasols have sticks, as well as handles, of ivory. By 1850, frames with metal stick and ferrule were being made, although this was not exactly new, for a metal stick is often found on the parasols of the early nineteenth century.

In parasols of the best quality the ribs were still made of whalebone during the 1840s; cane is found in the less expensive ones. Metal ribs of tubular steel were patented by Hollands of Birmingham in 1840 and re-designed by them in 1850. Fox's made solid steel ribs—mainly for umbrellas—in 1848, and patented U-section steel ribs in 1852. In 1851, metal frames were still more expensive than cane ones, so that the presence of cane ribs is as likely to be a sign of a less expensive parasol as a sign of early date. Whalebone ribs are rarely found after 1870.

The covers of the parasols were in all shades of silk. In 1849 there were: "all colours from plain green and brown to the most strong shades of pink, blue, etc.; some are of plain, others of figured silk, or figured only at the border. The more ornamental

39. Parasols, 1840–70

(above) *Grey silk, warp-printed in mauve, blue and brown, wooden stick and handle, the pagoda shape of the 1860s.*

(centre, left) *Black lace over white silk, ivory stick and folding ivory handle. The stick is hinged at the top so that the parasol can be tilted back parallel with the stick, a* marquise *parasol, 1850–65.*

(centre, right) *Red figured satin with short fringe, wooden stick and folding ivory handle, short carved ivory ferrule. 1840–50.*

(below) *White silk with printed border, edged with deep fringe, wooden stick and folding ivory handle, 1840–60.*

40. Blouse, hat and parasol, 1897
from an advertisement

The parasol shows the elaborate lining of the late 1890s. The hat, basically a sailor shape, with the brim tilted up at one side, the trimming of bows and feather rising above the crown in front, is, with its spotted veil, a characteristic hat of the late 1890s. The blouse has the high collar of the 1890s, and the puffed epaulettes at the shoulder, the last vestige of the leg-of-mutton sleeve, which are a particular fashion of this year, 1897. The wide belt worn over the junction of blouse and skirt is another fashionable detail of this decade.

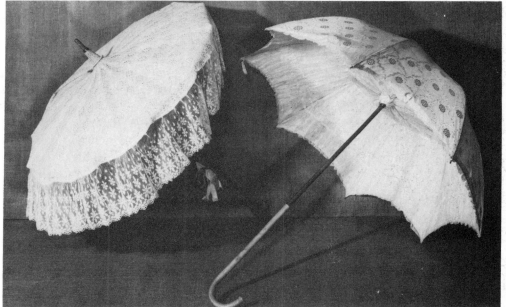

41. Parasols, 1880–1900
(left) *This parasol of cream openwork cotton over cream satin, with a deep awning of embroidered net has the usual shaping of parasols ofthe 1880s, a flat-topped pagoda with a thick wooden handle, here shaped like a beak, with a bow of ribbon attached.*

(right) *The white figured silk cover is lined with gathered silk muslin and shows one of the plainer versions of the parasols of the late 1890s.*

parasols suited to the carriage drive are trimmed with deep fringe or covered with guipure. For walking, plain parasols of rather larger size are preferred, but for the carriage those of somewhat smaller dimensions are found most convenient. The Marquise parasol, furnished with a hinge for turning the top on one side and with a folding stick, is peculiarly convenient for the carriage" (*Lady's Newspaper*, 1849). Some were covered in fabric which was specially woven or printed for parasol covers (Plate 39). The parasols were often lined, usually with white silk, although a lining was less general at the beginning of the period.

Parasols of plain silk covered with black or white lace were a fashion of the 1850s and early 1860s (Plate 39). "For occasions when a full-dress parasol is required nothing is so suitable and distinguished as black or white lace made up over a bright coloured or white parasol" (*Englishwoman's Domestic Magazine*, 1862). During the 1840s and 1850s, a deep fringe was usual as an awning (Plate 39); this disappeared in the 1860s. Parasols of checkered silk, with a band of the darkest shade in the check as a border, were "amongst the novelties of the season" in 1862. There are also examples of feather-covered or feather-trimmed parasols from this period.

There were two main shapes: the dome-shape usually found in the carriage parasol; and the shape in which the ribs were slightly flattened before tapering into the ferrule. This was usually called a Chinese top, or a pagoda shape, and was usually a style for plainer parasols. This shape was particularly popular between 1860 and 1865 (Plate 39), but is not limited to that period. Square parasols, also, are occasionally found.

During these years when parasols were much used, there were several devices to make their manipulation easier. Sangsters in 1844 patented the "Sylphide" parasol, which had a spring at the end of the handle so that the parasol could be closed with the hand which was holding it. The folding stick which is found on most of the parasols of this period had its origin earlier. The sticks are hinged and the joint held by a short ivory or metal tube which slides over it (Plate 39). A second hinge to make the parasol tilt back at the top of the stick, found on some of the parasols of the mid-nineteenth century (Plate 39), was also an inheritance from the earlier nineteenth century. The folding stick disappears in the 1860s, but the tilting top is occasionally found in parasols of the next period.

The parasols of the next generation lose the elegance and delicacy of the early Victorian examples. Already in 1861 "parasols are generally worn of a plain shape without any trimming and are rather large . . . to serve us as an umbrella as well as a parasol" (*Englishwoman's Domestic Magazine*, 1861). The new parasols in the shops in 1865 were described as "umbrella-shaped, rather large . . . a novelty in handles is their thickness" (*Queen*, 1865). By 1866 the change is complete. "The sticks are much shorter than formerly and the handles extremely thick" (*Queen*, 1866).

The handles continue short and thick during the 1870s but become longer, though still rather heavy, in the 1880s. Heads of animals and birds often decorate them in the 1870s and, in the 1880s, there are round-knobbed handles and natural knobbed ends of gnarled sticks of malacca briar, ash or vine. Large bows of ribbon decorate the handles in the 1870s and 1880s (Plate 41). The ferrules, like the handles, are slightly heavier in the 1860s, and then have a more definite change in the 1870s and 1880s. In the 1860s and early 1870s there are three types, a knob, a ring, and a stick; but in the late 1870s, the stick ferrule is general, and some parasols of this time have particularly long ones (Fig. 26).

Covers with ruched trimmings are a mark of the 1870s (Fig. 26). A deep lace awning is also an ornament of the 1870s and 1880s (Plate 41). Plain sunshades of silk with a border of contrasting colour are found at the same time as the more elaborate examples: "the *en-tout-cas* which is enjoying such wide popularity just now was never seen in so large a variety of designs both as regards the colouring, material and handles. . . . In the parasol proper there is a great variety of new shapes. The double triangle, treble triangle, pentagon and double pentagon, hexagons and octagons surmounted by their duplicate are all as novel as the new ideas embodied in their covers" (*Lady's World*, 1887).

In the late 1880s, parasols grow longer and appear slimmer when closed. The plainer parasols of the 1890s differ from those of the 1880s in their longer, lighter sticks and larger covers, which lie closely to the sticks when they are closed. The length of the sticks is usually between 36 and 40 inches, and the diameter of the cover between 24 and 35 inches. The corresponding sizes for the middle period of 1865 to 1885 have a length of 25 to 30 inches and a diameter of 20 to 25 inches; and, for the earlier period of 1835 to 1865, a length of 22 to 28 inches and a diameter of 16 to 22 inches. The silks are once more lighter and brighter, and

FIGURE 26.—PARASOLS AND SUNSHADES (*Milliner and Dressmaker, 1874*)

warp-printed designs are again fashionable. But the parasols of this period are to those of the 1840s as the peony to the pink. In 1896 attention is given to the lining, and for the next few years "Geisha" parasols with plain covers, but with linings of ruched and puffed chiffon or silk muslin are a characteristic fashion (Plate 40). The handles are a small knob on an extension of the stick. Decorative china handles are very popular at this time. The plainer sunshades for morning wear are contemporary with more elaborate examples, and both pass together into the next reign.

CHAPTER 19

MEN'S COSTUME

MEN'S garments of the Victorian period have survived in far less quantity than women's. Throughout the period, the dress of men was generally a suit composed of coat, waistcoat and trousers, not always of matching material. A coat or cloak was added for outdoor wear. At any time, two or three variations of each garment would be in general use for each occasion of wear. Then one variety would become dominant, the others continuing for some time as old-fashioned wear, or being relegated to a definite and more limited use.

Of these garments, trousers are the rarest survivors. Waistcoats survive in quantity, coats are not scarce, but trousers are more rarely found. At the beginning of the period, trousers had just become well-established for general wear and breeches had almost disappeared, except for their survival in court dress and for riding. Pantaloons, which were tight-fitting garments reaching the calf or ankle, had been worn since the beginning of the century and were still worn, particularly with evening dress; but narrow trousers, with straps under the instep, were taking their place, and pantaloons were seldom worn after 1850. The straps under the instep also disappeared in the early 1850s. For most of the period the trousers were narrow, with slight variation of width, but in the late 1850s and early 1860s the "peg-top" trouser (Fig. 27), wide at the top of the leg and tapering to the ankle, was a distinctive fashion. At the beginning of the period, a fall-front was still in use, but the fly front was becoming increasingly used, and was general by 1850. Knickerbockers, a loose form of breeches, appeared for sport and country wear in the 1860s and continued for this use until the end of the century.

The pantaloons and trousers for evening wear at the beginning of the period were black cloth, and black trousers continued to be the only style for evening wear to the end of the century. For

FIGURE 27.—THE LATEST FASHION (*Punch*, *1857*)

CHARLES.—"Sweet style of trowser, Gus!"

GUS.—"Ya-as! And so doosed comfortable. They're called **pantalons à la peg-top.**"

CHARLES.—"No!—really!"

(Reproduced by permission of *Punch*.)

daytime wear the trousers were usually of a contrasting colour to the coat (Plate 2); white, fawn or pale grey in a fine milled cloth were fashionable, and striped, checked and plaid materials for less formal wear. The stout cottons, nankeen and drill, were still used for summer wear, although they were less common after the middle of the century. The use of one material for coat, trousers and waistcoat appeared in the 1860s, particularly for the informal suit with the lounge jacket.

The frock coat was the usual coat form for day dress at the beginning of the reign. It was cut with a long waist and a short full skirt. It could be double-breasted or single-breasted. It was the dominant coat form for the 1840s and early 1850s and continued to be worn until the end of the century. During the 1840s, its fastening rose higher, shortening the lapels. The double-notched "M" lapel went out of fashion on frock coats by about 1850. In the 1860s, there was less shaping for the waist, and the sleeves were wider at the shoulder, tapering towards the wrist. The sleeves thus repeated the line of the "peg-top" trousers and showed the same wide shaped form as women's sleeves of the 1860s. By 1870 they had lost the shoulder fullness and were less shaped, falling straight to the wrist, where the cuff became more defined, closing with two buttons. The waistline rose in the 1890s and the lapels lengthened.

Although the frock coat was worn throughout the century, it lost its dominant position in the 1850s, when the morning coat began to replace it. A frock coat, with the skirt cut away in front in a curve from the waist, was worn as a riding coat in the 1830s and 1840s, and this shaping was adapted for a coat which gradually came into use as an alternative to the frock coat.

A jacket shorter than the frock coat or morning coat appeared by about 1850. Unlike these coats, it had visible pockets. It was a garment of informal wear for country or seaside, and it became general in the 1860s. Like the frock and morning coats, it had a sleeve wide at the shoulder and a straight loose line. It was made in both double-breasted and single-breasted forms. By the end of the 1860s, this jacket had also become accepted for general daytime wear. A belted form, with the jacket cut full and pleated back and front, was fashionable for country wear and was known as the Norfolk jacket. In the 1880s, the single-breasted forms had rounded fronts, a shaping which continued until the end of the century.

The tail coat, with fronts cut away to waist level, which had been a style for both day and evening wear before 1830, had by the beginning of the reign become mainly a style for evening wear. It still appeared for formal daytime wear in the 1840s, but by 1860 it was an evening style only, and it remained the style of evening dress to the end of the century and beyond. It could be single- or double-breasted. The evening dress form had long lapels revealing much of the waistcoat; the day dress coat, for as long as it was worn, had higher buttoning. The lapels were notched and the double "M" notch continued in the evening coat into the 1860s. In the 1880s a style with roll collar appeared as an alternative to the separate collar and lapel, the roll collar curving low to reveal a large expanse of shirt front; both styles were worn in the 1890s. Sleeves wide at the top, and tapering to the wrist, also appeared in these coats in the 1860s.

In the 1880s another type of coat appeared for the less formal evening occasions. It had the new roll collar of the tail coat of this decade, and the short form of the lounge jacket which had been adopted for day wear. By the end of the century it was known as a dinner jacket.

The evening coats were made of fine, milled cloth and from the beginning of the period were usually black or navy blue. Brown, dark green and mulberry colour might still appear but, by 1860, a black tail coat was the universal evening uniform. The frock coats were black, blue, brown or mulberry colour, but by far the greater number of surviving examples are black or blue. Most are a finely milled cloth, but they were made in twilled and other cloths. The lounge jacket had a much wider range of materials, including the lighter worsteds and tweeds. Dark grey was popular during the 1890s for all coats but the evening coat. Velvet collars appeared on dress and frock coats, particularly before 1860 (Plate 2). A fine cord edging is characteristic of coats from the beginning of the reign to about 1850.

Most of the colour and ornament of men's dress was concentrated in the waistcoat, a garment which has survived in larger

42. Silk Waistcoats, 1840–50
(left) *White silk figured in white and pale blue.*

(right) *Grey silk, figured in black, cream, red and green. Both have two tabs with metal eyelet holes threaded with tapes for lacing across the back.*

43. Embroidered waistcoat, 1835–45
Black satin embroidered in coloured silks in rose and convolvulus pattern. This has pairs of sewn-on tapes to tie across the back, an earlier method than the tabs and eyelet holes of the waistcoats of Plate 42.

44. Velvet waistcoat, 1845–55
Tartan check velvet in black, blue, red, green, yellow and white, with horizontal tripes in silk twill. The lacing at the back is from tabs with eyelet holes as in the waistcoats of Plate 42.

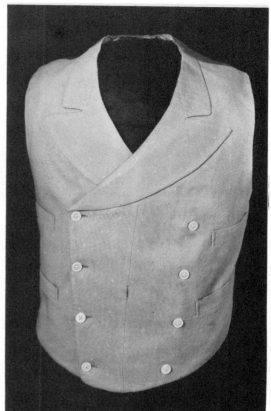

45.   Cotton plush and wool waistcoats, 1879 and 1885
(left) *Blue plush, worn at a wedding in 1885*

(right) *Fawn wool with small star pattern in cream and orange silk, with a slit for the watch chain in the front seam, worn at a wedding in 1879. Both have straps and metal buckle at the back.*

quantities than any other man's garment of this period. Until the 1860s it showed the fabrics and colours and the woven and printed designs fashionable in the materials of women's dress. The tradition of embroidery for waistcoats, much of it now by the amateur, continued (Fig. 28). The type of fabric and the degree of ornament depended on the occasion of wearing, but until the 1860s the waistcoat was usually in definite but harmonizing contrast to coat and trousers, not only in colour but in the texture of its material (Plate 2). The higher fastening of coats, particularly the lounge jacket in the 1860s and 1870s, concealed much of the waistcoat, and this and the development of the wearing of coat, waistcoat and trousers of the same material, or coat and waistcoat alike with contrasting trousers, or trousers and waistcoat alike with contrasting coat, meant the eclipse of the waistcoat. "Fancy" waistcoats were revived in the 1890s, but beside the sure harmony or vivid splendour of the 1840s and 1850s their fancy appears hesitant and characterless (Plate 45).

Many of the waistcoats which survive have been preserved because they were wedding waistcoats. These were often in white or cream figured silk, or white silk embroidered, although many examples have survived as wedding waistcoats which do not follow this fashion. For evening wear, also, the waistcoat was often white, in many different kinds of silk at the beginning of the period, but black evening waistcoats were fashionable in the 1860s and 1870s; only in the 1890s did white marcella or piqué become the usual wear, the black waistcoat remaining with the dinner jacket. In the 1840s, the dress waistcoats of day wear and informal evening wear were in figured silks and satins very like the fabrics of women's dress at the time (Plate 42). Plain silks and satins were embroidered, usually in a bordering pattern and on the pockets (Fig. 28). At the beginning of the period, the liking for bright patterns on a dark background which appeared in women's aprons, bags and shawls, appeared also in waistcoats, with cross-stitch patterns in brightly coloured silks on a black or dark satin ground (Plate 43). Fine white or black twilled wool was also used and embroidered. In the 1850s, there was an increasing fashion for tartan patterning in silk and velvet and the colours grew brighter in daytime wear (Plate 44). Although

examples of dress waistcoats in figured velvets and similar
materials survive from all periods up to the last years of the
century, there was, after 1860, much less use of silk, particularly
for daytime wear, and even when waistcoats did not match the
cloth of coat and trousers, they were often in a woollen fabric
with pattern limited to a fancy weave in a single colour.

The waistcoats of the 1840s often show a pointed, rather long
waistline. In the 1850s, the fronts were slightly cut away, forming

FIGURE 28.—EMBROIDERY FOR A GENTLEMAN'S WAISTCOAT
(*Lady's Newspaper, 1849*)
Embroidery in silk on satin or cashmere.

a small triangular gap at the centre waist. In the late 1860s, the
waistline became shorter and the line at the waist was less pointed
and nearer the horizontal. This movement of shortening and

straightening at the waist kept in time with the more conspicuously changing line in women's dress. The waistcoat lengthened a little in the 1870s and 1880s, but generally kept the horizontal line until the 1890s, when the day waistcoat again showed a small gap at the centre waist.

In the 1840s, the single-breasted form was general, although the double-breasted form appeared, particularly in plainer examples for daytime wear. For day wear, double-breasted forms increased in popularity during the 1850s and 1860s. The single-breasted form was more usual for evening wear throughout the period until the last years of the century, and particularly before 1870. For day wear, both types were worn to the end of the century. There were usually two pockets, sometimes three, until 1870; then three were usual and four occasional. Crescent-shaped pockets on waistcoats are usually a sign of an 1830s or 1840s date.

The neck opening at the beginning of the period often had the collar continuous with the lapel, the opening being wide and deep; during the 1850s, the fastening rose a little higher and there were a larger proportion of waistcoats with a separate collar and lapel, the lapels often being wider and shorter; but the earlier form remained in fashion, particularly for evening wear. Waistcoats buttoning high, with or without a collar but without lapels, were worn in the 1860s. A deep opening appeared again in the 1870s, mainly in double-breasted styles. In the single-breasted styles, the fastening was higher and the collar and lapels were small, or there might be no collar. A higher fastening was general on all waistcoats in the 1890s except evening waistcoats, on which the opening widened and deepened in the 1880s and 1890s.

At the beginning of the period the back of the waistcoat was usually tightened by tapes threaded through tabs sewn at the back. The tapes might be sewn directly on to the waistcoat back, but this was a survival of the eighteenth-century style, which was going out of use by 1840. Tabs which have metal eyelet holes all fall within the period. After 1845, the ties were being replaced by a strap and buckle, although the older method continued in use for many years. Leather facings were used at the base of the waistcoat fronts in the late 1840s and early 1850s. Darts under the lapels appeared mostly in waistcoats of the 1840s. The back and lining were usually of glazed cotton, but silk was sometimes used for evening waistcoats. Linings of striped cotton appeared in waistcoats for day wear from the 1860s. At the beginning of the period, and until about 1850, underwaistcoats were sometimes worn, to show at the opening of the waistcoat. These, which were a continued fashion from the 1820s and 1830s, were either collar and lapels only, or a short waistcoat.

Linen shirts with a high collar and frilled opening were still being worn at the beginning of the period, and the frill remained on evening shirts until about 1850, when it was gradually replaced by a front section of vertical tucking or pleating, the opening being fastened by buttons or studs. This fastening was already used for shirts of day wear from the beginning of the period. A small frill sometimes remained round the vertical section containing the buttons and buttonholes, which was a decorative feature of shirts in the 1850s and 1860s. After 1870, shirt fronts became plain. Shirts with decorated fronts sometimes had a back fastening, and some a side fastening. After 1850, the corners of the shirt, where the seam opened at the base, were rounded. Striped cotton shirts were used for sporting and country wear from the beginning of the period, but not until the last years of the century were coloured shirts accepted for formal day wear.

The collar became lower during the 1840s and 1850s, when it began to turn down over the cravat. Detachable collars were worn from this time, and collar and cuffs and shirt front show an increasing stiffness in the second half of the nineteenth century. Collars with ends high in front were worn in the 1850s, but the collars of the 1860s and 1870s were low. They were now either single or double, the double being used only for daytime wear. The single collars were upright, with a gap at the centre front, or with the corners turned down. After 1880, the collar in all forms grew higher and, for most of the 1890s, was between two and a half and three inches high. This high collar appeared in both men's and women's dress in the 1890s.

In the late 1830s, the neckcloth or cravat was still a piece of white muslin, folded into a band, wrapped round the neck in front and brought from back to front again to tie in a great variety of knots. Black silk was becoming increasingly worn for daytime, and also coloured silk both plain and figured. A stiffened, made-up band, with or without a bow in front, was also worn. It was then called a stock. By the end of the 1840s, white was unusual except for evening wear. After a period in the 1840s when black cravats were fashionable for evening wear, white remained usual for full evening dress for all the rest of the period, whatever the shaping of the cravat or tie. There was a change in the tying of the cravat in the 1840s, when the neck band was made narrow and the bow or knot very large (Fig. 29). The cravat was sometimes knotted loosely as a scarf, fitting the opening of the waistcoat and fixed by a pin (Plate 2). By 1860, the collar of the shirt had become much lower and was turning down in front. The cravat was now a narrow band of material, usually less than an inch wide, tied in a small flat bow in front or knotted and fixed by a pin. These very narrow ties are characteristic of the 1850s and 1860s. The tie now made as a shaped band, narrow in the centre for the neck, wider at the ends, was tied in a bow or knot during the 1870s and 1880s. In the 1890s, when the collar became higher, many varieties of knot and a great variety of materials were used in ties.

One of the most decorative accessories of men's dress during the period was its braces. Braces of canvas, embroidered in coloured silks and lined with silk, were fashionable in the 1830s and 1840s. Later they were embroidered in wool. They were made in two separate bands, with leather tabs with buttonholes, one end adjustable with a buckle. Braces joined at the back appeared in the second half of the century, but directions for making braces of the earlier pattern still appeared in magazines of the 1860s. "Braces form a necessary adjunct to a gentleman's wardrobe and they are generally pleased to have them prettily worked" (*Englishwoman's Domestic Magazine* (*Patterns, Fashions and Needlework*, 1865). Braces were also made in knitted and crocheted cotton.

Outdoor coats and capes for men are rather rare survivors. The cloak was still worn for evening, but became less general after the 1860s, although never completely out of fashion. Short cloaks and short-sleeved capes were also worn in the 1850s and 1860s. One of these which became much used, particularly for

FIGURE 29.—(*Punch, 1853*)

FIRST COCK SPARROW.—"What a miwackulous Tye, Fwank! How the doose do you manage it?"

SECOND COCK SPARROW.—"Yas, I fancy it is rather grand; but then you see, I give the whole of my mind to it!"

(Reproduced by permission of *Punch.*)

travelling, was the Inverness cape, a coat with wide sleeves, with a cape added. From the 1870s, these sometimes had the same dolman-sleeve forms as women's mantles at this time, the cape ending at the sides, and forming the sleeves. The frock coat was worn as an overcoat, with variations, throughout the period, but the overcoat most generally fashionable throughout the reign was the Chesterfield. This had no waist seam and was straighter and looser than the frock coat. At the beginning of the period it had slight shaping for the waist, but became straighter after 1860. There were both single- and double-breasted forms and also, after 1850, a style with concealed front fastening. There were also short coats, the lounge jackets of outdoor wear. Those of the 1850s and 1860s were distinguished by very large buttons, a characteristic which was borrowed with these jacket forms by women's dress (Fig. 14). Overcoats of the 1860s also showed the wide, shaped sleeve, a characteristic detail of this decade which is found in the dress of both men and women. The raglan sleeve, cut up to the neck on the shoulder, appeared in overcoats in the late 1850s and 1860s and was again fashionable in the late 1890s. The short coat of the 1880s and 1890s was the covert coat, which was a short Chesterfield, with concealed front fastenings. A very long, belted overcoat, the Ulster, appeared in the 1870s and was particularly popular as a travelling coat. In the 1890s, it was usually worn with a half-belt at the back only. The full-length coats varied in fashionable length, ending as high as the knee, or as low as mid-calf, until the 1890s, when all coats lengthened to end between calf and ankle. The heavier milled cloths and tweeds were used for these outdoor coats, mainly in black, dark blue, grey and brown shades.

The top hat, with a high, flat-topped crown and narrow brim, was worn throughout the reign. At the beginning of the period the crown was high, about seven or eight inches, and the sides curved out slightly at the top; the narrow brim curved up slightly at the sides. This hat was worn for all occasions in silk, beaver, felt and straw, in black, fawn, grey or white. A collapsible form was in use for evening wear. A lower-crowned, broader-brimmed style was worn in the country and unfashionably.

During the 1850s, the silk form of the top hat became dominant, and the low-crowned hats were usually of felt or straw. Straight-brimmed straw hats, the sailor shape of the time, appeared for informal summer wear (Plate 6), and a round cloth cap was also worn for sport and in the country. A new form, the bowler, or round-crowned, hard felt hat, was added to the hats of informal wear in the 1860s (Plate 6). In the 1870s, a hat with dented crown and curving brim, which later, in the 1890s, was given the name of "Trilby", also appeared in soft felt and straw. The most popular informal hat of the 1890s was the straw boater, a stiffened straw with flat, round crown and straight brim. A development from the sailor shape of the middle of the century, it entered informal town wear by way of tennis and boating in the 1880s. The deerstalker cap, a cap in tweed with flaps which could be tied over the ears or over the top of the cap, was a country and sporting fashion of the 1880s and 1890s. There were also a number of variants of the main types of hat, such as a flat-top bowler, a stiff trilby—known as the Homburg—and a tweed helmet, with peaks at the back and front.

The top hat remained tall until the mid-1860s, when its crown lowered to about six inches. In the 1880s, the crown of this hat, and that of the bowler—which was worn with lounge suits— became higher; but in the 1890s, both were lower again. For all formal wear, with frock coat, morning coat and evening dress, the high hat remained fashionable until the end of the century. For less formal town wear the bowler, usually also black, was the main style. Brown, grey and fawn appeared in the softer felts and, as a sign of summer, in the bowler. Dark and speckled plaits were used in straw hats, although the natural-coloured straw was the more general fashion.

High boots, reaching just below the knee with a curving top, were known as Hessians, and with a straight plain top as Wellingtons. These still continued in wear for walking, but the shorter half-boot forms were more usual. The commonest form of the half-boot was the Blucher, a half-length Wellington, with front lacing. From 1837, boots with elastic gussets at the side were worn, and men also wore boots with leather toes and cloth tops, with side lacing, matching those worn by women. After 1850, long boots disappeared except for riding. The leather and cloth boots with side lacing also disappeared, but the elastic-sided boot continued to be worn and did not entirely disappear from old-fashioned use until the end of the century. Button boots, which had appeared in the late 1830s, became fairly common in the 1860s, and they were particularly fashionable in the 1870s and

1880s. The front lacing boots from the late 1860s might have metal hooks instead of holes at the top, to hold the laces.

At the beginning of the period, there were two types of shoe: one the dress shoe, which was a light low-heeled pump with a low front; and the other a shoe with latchets and lacing over the front, which was low-heeled but still suggestive of the style of the eighteenth century. In the late 1840s, a shoe with lacing up the front appeared. Buttoned shoes came into use with buttoned boots in the 1860s and were worn during the 1870s and 1880s. Boots were, however, still the usual wear until the end of the century.

Boots and shoes were square-toed, and rather long and narrow in shape at the beginning of the reign. They became wider in the 1860s; at the same time the toe rounded a little, and then during the 1880s became pointed. This change of shaping came to the boots and shoes of men and women alike.

Stockings were usually knee-length at the beginning of the period. They were white, black, speckled or striped, and were made of silk, wool or cotton. During the century they grew shorter. Gaiters might be worn in the country in the first half of the period, and short gaiters or spats, which covered the ankle only, were fashionable town wear from the 1870s to the end of the century.

The fashions of men are more influenced by the occasion of wearing, less by the precise moment of time at which they are worn, than women's. Evening dress preserved the early coat style with square cut-away front to the end of the period and beyond. Riding dress also kept this form until the 1850s. The early nineteenth-century coat with curving cut-away, known as the Newmarket coat, was, on the other hand, used first for riding, and then in the 1850s came into use as the morning coat. For riding, trousers of white cord were much worn in the first half of the period; for hunting, breeches continued to be used. The hunting coat was usually a short frock coat of scarlet cloth, although green was still worn at the beginning of the period. Shooting jackets were, at first, short frock coats, and then the shorter lounge jacket. Both forms are distinguished by a number of visible pockets. The Norfolk jacket was also a fashion for shooting in the 1860s and, unlike the lounge jacket, never left the country. For cricket and tennis, short jackets with patch pockets were worn. These jackets, which were often brightly coloured and by the 1890s were known as blazers, also remained limited to sporting wear. The habit of smoking also produced its jacket, a loose lounge jacket, usually of velvet or heavy silk, sometimes quilted and trimmed with silk cord. Smoking jackets were worn from the 1850s until the end of the century. A smoking cap was sometimes worn with a smoking jacket; this was a round flat cap, made in the pork-pie shape of velvet, silk or cloth, braided or embroidered and often with a tassel. Illustrations for making and decorating these caps appear frequently in fashion journals of the second half of the century, and the caps, many obviously unworn, survive in quantity.

CHAPTER 20

CHILDREN'S COSTUME

THE dress of children—that is, boys and girls between the ages of three and sixteen—was related in different ways to adult fashion. It often reflected in miniature the adult fashions of its day. The dress of girls from the beginning of the reign to the 1890s was mostly a series of smaller, simpler versions of the styles worn by their mothers. It did, however, at times, lead, not follow, adult fashion. The hat styles of the mid-nineteenth century were worn first by boys and girls, then by younger women, and finally were accepted into fashionable wear. It also had styles and garments of its own, which were peculiar to childhood. The dress of boys diverged more from the dress of their fathers than that of girls from their mothers. The tunics worn by boys in the middle of the nineteenth century, and the visible ankle-length drawers of little girls at the beginning of the period, were fashions of children only.

Dress of Children Under Five

Small boys and girls up to the age of five or six were dressed very much alike. Boys as well as girls wore short frocks, with low neckline and short sleeves. Many of these frocks were made of white cotton. In the 1850s and 1860s, they had a full skirt and were embroidered in the large white openwork known as *broderie anglaise*. Dresses of this kind survive in some quantity. They were worn with bows of ribbon on the shoulder and sashes, sometimes round the waist, sometimes over the shoulder. White embroidered dresses continued to be worn in the 1870s and 1880s. The influence of the changing lines of women's dress can be seen, especially in the princess front, formed by a panel of embroidery, and in the pleating at the centre back of the skirt. Children of three or four might still have a low neckline, although this was generally higher than in the 1850s and 1860s; and they also still

46. Contemporary photograph showing boy's dress and jacket, 1868
The dress and matching jacket, probably of velvet, were worn by a boy of four. The white embroidered ends of drawers are visible beneath the dress. The round hat has a fur band round the turned-back brim.

47.　Contemporary photograph showing a girl wearing a crinoline, 1860–5
The skirt of her dress is obviously supported by a crinoline frame. The matching three-quarter length jacket shows a fashionable shaping in its sleeve.

48.   Contemporary photograph showing boys' suits, 1860–70
The jackets of these suits with long trousers fasten at the neck with a single button. The sleeve just reveals the fashionable line of the 1860s, which is seen in its more emphatic form in Plate 47.

49. Contemporary photograph showing boys' sailor suits and girl's dress, 1882–6
The two boys show sailor suits of the 1880s. All three have long dark stockings and the elder boy has metal hooks to finish off the lacing of his boots. The high neckline and the tight sleeves ending above the wrist link the girl's dress with the fashions of the early 1880s. The tam-o-shanter *hat was a popular style for girls and small boys in the 1880s.*

50. Boy's dress of tartan check wool, 1873–4
The material is a woollen twill checked in red, green, blue, black and yellow (Royal Stuart tartan). The embroidered frills of drawers were still often visible in the dress of small boys.

51.   Girl's dress, wool and silk, 1875
The dress is in fawn and grey shot silk and grey twilled wool and in this use of two different materials and its polonaise bodice, with basque, and apron front over a separate skirt, and its pleated frills it is a miniature of adult fashion of this time. It was originally worn by a child of four and a half.

wore very short sleeves until the 1890s, although for children of four or five sleeves were generally longer. For harder wear, white piqué was also used, trimmed with braid or with embroidered insertions and frills. Plaid dresses for boys and girls under six were also fashionable from the beginning of the period up to the 1870s (Plate 50). Examples survive in many different materials, including silk, poplin and woollen fabrics. Silk was used for best dresses; and velvet and striped and checked woollen materials were much used for small boys (Plate 46). There are a number of surviving dresses in black corded silk and black poplin, in very small sizes, showing that children of this age were dressed in mourning.

Frocks worn by small boys can sometimes be distinguished from those of girls by the pleating of the skirt. "Little boys do not wear any crinolines even while in petticoats and their skirts are not gored, but arranged in flat pleats overlapping one another" (*Englishwoman's Domestic Magazine*, 1866). A number of the frocks were made with matching jackets (Plate 46). Frocks not made of white cotton usually had white collar and cuffs. The legs of white cotton, or linen drawers, long and tubular, reached to the ankle at the beginning of the period, but became wider and shorter and frilled during the 1840s and 1850s, and were disappearing during the 1860s (Plate 46).

Hats of straw or beaver, with round crowns and broad brims, were worn by small children in the 1840s. Boys often had flat caps with a peak and tassel. In the 1860s, children's hats showed a great variety of shaping, but flat round hats with turned-up brim were particularly popular and were worn by children of all ages (Plate 46). There was very little difference between the hats worn by boys and girls. A small round hat of velvet trimmed with a tuft of feathers is as likely to have been worn by a boy as a girl. White felt hats trimmed with bright blue or cerise were regarded as particularly suitable for small children. For summer wear there were straw hats, bound with ribbon and trimmed with rosettes or tufts of feathers. A narrow-brimmed straw hat was still worn in the 1870s, and the soft, flat-crowned, tam-o'-shanter became popular then and was much worn in the 1880s by boys and girls alike. The broad-brimmed sailor hat with upturned brim was worn in the 1880s and 1890s. Soft-crowned bonnets were also worn by girls, usually with a halo-like brim.

Small children wore shoes, usually with ankle straps and these changed very little in shape through the century; but they also wore short buttoned boots. Socks, mostly of white cotton, were worn by the very young from the beginning of the period and, by the 1880s, socks were generally worn by children under seven.

Boys

At the beginning of the period, small boys of five put on long trousers when they left off their frocks. With the trousers they wore a short round jacket, a short jacket and waistcoat, or a longer tunic. This was a short jacket with a skirt, like the skirted coat worn by men. After 1850, the short jacket was the usual form. It had slight basques in the 1840s and 1850s, but became shorter and was open in front, fastening only at the neck, like the Zouave jacket of women's fashion. This style was general during the 1860s (Plate 48). For everyday wear, the younger boys wore blouses, that is, a loose tunic of holland or cashmere, usually with a belt and sometimes with a diagonal fastening.

In the 1860s, knickerbocker suits replaced trousers for younger boys and were worn by boys between the ages of three and ten. The knickerbockers either hung straight—the trousers cut short— or they were gathered at the knee. They were worn with the same style of jacket. "Little boys wear jackets in preference to frocks from the age of three or four. Up to seven years old the jacket is open over a full white shirt with frills; after that a waistcoat is worn. The trousers are full and wide and either straight or gathered in at the knee. After the boy has outgrown white piqué and brown holland, nothing is more suitable than a suit of grey cloth or cashmere with no ornament but braid and gimp buttons of the same colour" (*Englishwoman's Domestic Magazine*, 1866). The full knickerbockers gathered at the knee went out of fashion in the 1880s, but the straight knee-length form remained and a fitted breeches-like form was also worn. The short trousers were worn up to the age of ten; after that long trousers were usual.

The short open jacket was replaced by longer jackets in the 1870s, either a long fitted one with a single- or double-breasted fastening, or a belted jacket, the type which was also adopted ior men's informal, outdoor wear at this time and known as a Norfolk jacket. The Eton suit, in which the short jacket and waistcoat of the early nineteenth century had been preserved, with its rival version, the Harrow suit, in which the jacket was pointed at the back, were generally worn by schoolboys in the 1880s and 1890s, with a wide, turn-down collar, also an Eton fashion, bearing its name. Cloth, tweed and cashmere were all used for boys' suits, and also velvet and plush. Fauntleroy suits in velvet with lace collars were a fashion of the 1880s and 1890s. The cloth suits were usually in grey, fawn, brown or blue, but the velvet suits were often in brighter colours. From 1850 to 1880, braid was constantly used as a trimming on cloth suits, with arabesque and geometric patterns in the 1860s but more often as a braided edging in the 1870s.

The jersey which, in machine-knitted fabric in silk or wool, was worn by women in the late 1870s, particularly for tennis, was also worn by small boys. It had an occupational ancestor in the knitted jerseys of fishermen and others who worked along the sea coasts, and knitted jerseys were occasionally worn by boys in the 1860s and 1870s. They became more popular in the 1880s. "Jersey costumes both for boys and girls will be more popular than ever this year; indeed these and washing dresses are the only costumes worn by children for ordinary wear. . . . Jersey costumes are better for boys than girls, though equally comfortable for both. . . . Besides being very pretty they are very healthy suits; they do not impede the boy's movements . . . they are cool, they admit the air, and yet being woollen they keep the body in a due state of warmth and prevent all chills" (*Myra's Journal*, 1884).

The Scotch or Highland suit was also fashionable for younger boys, particularly in the late 1860s and 1870s. It usually had a pleated skirt, not necessarily in a tartan material, jacket and Scotch cap.

It was, however, the Navy which had the greatest influence on boys' dress in the second half of the period. Sailor costumes appeared amongst children's fashions from the late 1850s and, by the 1880s, the sailor suit had developed as a definite style for boys, and remained a much worn style until the end of the century (Plate 49). It was made in navy blue serge for winter, and in white cotton drill for summer, with both blouse and jacket forms and short and long trousers. It was worn with sailor hats, at first a flat-crowned, narrow-brimmed hat, but, by the 1880s, a round straw with turned up brim or a round cloth cap were usual. To complete the illusion, the hats often had a band bearing the name of a ship.

At the beginning of the period, the peaked flat-crowned cap was worn by boys to about the age of ten, before they wore tall hats in the style of their fathers. The other styles worn by children under five throughout the period, the narrow-brimmed hats with rather large flat crowns, sailor hats of different kinds and tam-o'-shanters, were also worn by boys a few years older, before they wore small versions of the straw boaters, bowler hats or tall hats of adult fashion. A round cap, made in sections and fitting the head, with a peak, which was originally worn for football and cricket, was schoolboy wear in the 1890s.

Girls

The dress of girls at the beginning of the reign had the lengthening and pointed waistline and the full skirt of women's fashion. The trimming often made the same V-shaped lines over the bodice. The skirt was shorter, ending well above the ankles for the younger children, and, because of this, young girls had their legs covered to the ankle by white drawers. At the beginning of the period, these were still narrow and tubular, and usually rather plain. During the 1840s and 1850s, they became wider and more ornamented with frills of openwork embroidery, but shorter and less visible beneath the hem of the dress. The length of the dress, in the first half of the period, varied according to age but, for most girls, it was never shorter than just below the knee, or longer than the top of the boot. The skirts of dresses in the 1850s were often flounced and some girls wore small crinolines beneath their skirts in the late 1850s and 1860s (Plate 47). Sleeves at the beginning of the period were often very short; but there are examples of long sleeves which buttoned on to shorter ones, a device not limited to children's dress of the time. The neckline was often very low on the shoulder. Many dresses of the 1850s and 1860s have a matching cape or jacket. In the 1860s, skirts and blouses were worn. "Children under seven years of age wear full Garibaldi shirts or *chemises Russes*, in white cambric, foulard or alpaca, embroidered in white or black with coloured skirts. But for ladies this style of dress is considered quite *négligé*, and can only be worn at home and for the morning" (*Englishwoman's Domestic Magazine*, 1863).

The dress of girls continued to follow that of women during the 1870s and 1880s, showing in miniature the overskirts, the looped and bustle effects of the early 1870s, the straight-fronted dress with pleating and bows at the centre back in the early 1880s. It followed adult fashion in more than line. There was the same use of two materials, the mingling of wool and silk, the same trimming of pleated frills (Plate 51). The very low neckline, except for young children, disappeared after the 1860s and from the late 1870s, girls' day dress had the same high neckline, with standing collar, as women's dress. Some garments and forms of adult dress were, however, not adopted. "Children's dresses and coats continue to be made in imitation of the costumes of older folk, only as yet they have not taken to the graceful Dolman" (*Ladies' Treasury*, 1881). There were other forms and details with a limited use in adult dress which were adopted in girls' dress and developed as a children's fashion.

During the 1880s, girls began to wear loose dresses, falling full from the shoulder or a yoke, and held by a belt or gathered into a band at the waist. These, like the loose tunics of the boys, were called blouses. This became the style of the 1890s, a dress more closely related to the needs of childhood than girls had enjoyed since the beginning of the century, and less closely related to adult fashion.

Many of these blouses or blouse dresses were smocked. In 1880, the *Queen* stated that "smocking, so popular one or two years ago for lawn tennis costume has now found its way into children's dress". Smocking, a technique of construction and ornament combined, was, of course, older than the tennis dress of the 1870s. It had developed in its most ornamental and conspicuous form in the round frocks of linen and cotton worn by countrymen during the nineteenth century, which could still be seen in use in 1880, although they were fast disappearing. From this time, it has been a continuous fashion for young children's dress, particularly girls, up to the present day. The smocked dresses worn by children in the 1880s resembled the countryman's frock and, because of this likeness, they had the nickname "Hodge".

Children of all periods have worn some kind of apron or pinafore to protect their dresses, but pinafores were particularly a fashion of the last twenty years of the period. In the 1880s and 1890s, pinafores, often in white muslin, trimmed with insertions and frills of white embroidery, were much worn. They often had a central panel of embroidery in the 1880s. In the 1890s, a yoked style was more usual, and sometimes the waistline was marked by an insertion. The more elaborate pinafores were threaded with ribbon.

In spite of the frills and embroidery of the pinafores, the dress of girls in the 1880s tended to draw closer to the dress of their brothers and was less a replica of their mothers fashions.

Girls as well as boys wore the jersey dress and they came under the influence of the Navy and wore sailor costumes. These might be practical blouses and skirts for rough wear at the seaside, or they might be more fashionable and elaborate costumes. "Sailor suits for boys and girls are just now much in vogue and will be so until the end of October; and for a more dressy style for girls, the man-of-war suits made of finest serge are braided with gold and silver braid" (*Ladies' Treasury*, 1883). The skirts were always pleated and were worn with a blouse or jacket, which had the large sailor collar. Serge, cashmere, or a stout cotton in white or navy blue, were the usual materials for them. Serge was a popular material for girls dress, for hard wear, at the end of the century.

White cotton or muslin, with openwork embroidery, was used for girls' dress all through the period. White cotton piqué and cotton satin were used for harder wear. Cotton printed with small sprigged designs appeared in children's dress in the 1840s and 1850s, when this type of pattern was no longer fashionable for adults. Alpaca, mohair and poplin were much used in the 1860s. Silk was also used for party wear. Striped and checked materials were used during most of the period for children, and plaids were particularly popular between 1850 and 1880. "Although plaid materials are no longer much employed for ladies' dresses, they are still generally chosen for children's costumes" (*Englishwoman's Domestic Magazine*, 1864). Velvet was much used as a trimming on the silk and woollen dresses, but the most popular form of trimming for children's dress was braid, which is found on a large proportion of dresses between 1840 and 1880. The combination of black braid with white piqué is often found in dresses of the 1860s: "Frocks and capes for young children are more than ever arranged for braiding, no other ornament having been found as yet so suitable for the purpose" (*Englishwoman's Domestic Magazine*, 1864).

During the 1840s, little girls wore bonnets, small replicas of those worn by their mothers, but during the 1850s they tested out the new fashions in hats. The "Pamela" hat, a broad-brimmed straw hat of 1855, was "first worn only by children and young ladies, but they are now being adopted by ladies of all ages" (*Englishwoman's Domestic Magazine*, 1865). In the 1860s, both boys and girls wore small round felt hats with turned-up brims; but there were many varieties of hat at this time. Some had cone-shaped crowns and narrow flat brims, or brims turned up at one side. The higher crown continued in the 1870s, and until the end of the century the shapes of girls' hats continually followed those of women's fashion; very small girls often wore hats differing little in style and trimming from their mothers'. In the 1880s, the flat-crowned beret or tam-o'-shanter was popular particularly for tennis. In the winter, round fur caps were worn. M. Vivian Hughes in *A London Child of the Seventies* (1934) remembers: "My outdoor clothes in winter never varied; a hat of real sealskin that stood all weathers and could not wear out, neither could it blow off, for it was fastened round my chin by elastic; my warmth was secured by a "cross-over", a strip of tartan about two yards long that crossed over in front and behind, leaving my arms free. The worst worry in going out was my boots which came far above the ankle with endless buttons that needed a button hook to do them up". In the 1890s, white cotton hats with large flat crowns and soft frilled brims were worn for many summers.

Short boots, buttoning at the sides, were usually worn, except by very small children. A boot with front fastening, shaped and tasselled at the front, was worn from 1863 until the late 1870s. By the 1890s, shoes fastened with lacing were beginning to be worn. White stockings were general for the first half of the period, although striped stockings, horizontally banded in colour, appeared in the 1860s. Black stockings became more general in the 1880s. With them, fine wool took the place of cotton: "Ribbed cashmere stockings for children have almost superseded cotton" (*Lady's World*, 1887).

APPENDIX

The following museums contain the main collections of Victorian dress or specialized collections relating to it although some of them are unable to present a full range on permanent display. A number of other museums have small collections.

Barnard Castle, Bowes Museum
Bath, Museum of Costume, Assembly Rooms
Birmingham, City Museum and Art Gallery
Brighton, Royal Pavilion Art Gallery and Museum
Bristol, City Museum and Art Gallery, Blaise Castle
Cardiff, National Museum of Wales, Welsh Folk Museum, St Fagans
Cheltenham, Art Gallery and Museum
Colchester and Essex Museum, The Hollytrees
Douglas, The Manx Museum, Library and Art Gallery
Edinburgh: National Museum of Antiquities of Scotland
        Royal Scottish Museum and Shambellie House, New Abbey, Dumfries
Exeter, Royal Albert Memorial Museum
Glasgow, Museums and Art Galleries, Aikenhead House
Halifax, Bankfield Museum
Hereford City Museum and Art Gallery, Churchill Gardens Museum
Hereford and Worcester County Museum, Hartlebury Castle
Ipswich, Museums and Art Galleries, Christchurch Mansion
Leeds: City Museum, Kirkstall Abbey
    City Art Galleries, Lotherton Hall, Aberford
Leicestershire Museums, Leicester, Wygston's House Museum of Costume (also collections illustrating the boot and shoe, hosiery and corset industries)
Liverpool, Merseyside County Museums
London: Victoria and Albert Museum and Bethnal Green Museum
        Museum of London
Luton Museum and Art Gallery (collection illustrating the hat industry)
Maidstone, Museum and Art Gallery
Manchester City Art Galleries, Gallery of English Costume, Platt Hall
Newcastle, Laing Art Gallery
Northampton Central Museum and Art Gallery (collection illustrating the boot and shoe industry)
Norwich Museums, Strangers Hall (also collections illustrating the shawl and boot and shoe industries)

Nottingham, Museum of Costume and Textiles, Castlegate
Paisley Museum and Art Gallery (collection illustrating the shawl industry)
Preston, Harris Museum and Art Gallery
Salisbury, Salisbury and South Wiltshire Museum
Taunton, Somerset County Museum
Warwick, Warwickshire County Museum
Worthing, Museum and Art Gallery
York, Castle Museum
A large private collection is shown at Castle Howard, Yorkshire and a collection belonging to the National Trust at Killerton House, Devon.
The Snowshill collection also belonging to the National Trust has been transferred to Blickling Hall for cataloguing and care and is not at present (1984) being shown to the public.

BIBLIOGRAPHY

FASHION MAGAZINES:

La Belle Assemblée.
The World of Fashion.
The Court Magazine.
The Ladies' Cabinet of Fashion.
The Ladies' Gazette of Fashion.
The Ladies' Companion.
The Lady's Newspaper.
The Queen.
The Englishwoman's Domestic Magazine.
The Ladies' Treasury.
The Young Ladies' Journal.
The Young Englishwoman.
Sylvia's Home Journal.
The Milliner and Dressmaker.

Myra's Journal.
The Lady's World.
Woman's World.
Woman at Home.
The Lady's Realm.
The Lady.
The Gentlewoman.
The Lady's Pictorial.
Weldon's Ladies' Journal.
Weldon's Home Dressmaker.
Weldon's Illustrated Dressmaker.
Weldon's Practical Needlework Series.
Tailor and Cutter.
West End Gazette of Gentlemen's Fashions.

OTHER PERIODICALS:

The Graphic.
The Illustrated London News.
Punch.

CONTEMPORARY WRITINGS:

Walker, G. *The Tailor's Masterpiece* (4th Edition, c. 1837).
The Workwoman's Guide by a Lady, 1838.
The Art of Dress or Guide to the Toilette, 1839.

The Ladies' Knitting and Netting Book, 1839.

Good, T., and Barnett, G. *Scientific Cutting Simplified*, 1845.

Howell, Mrs. M. J. *Handbook of Millinery*, 1847.

Elegant Arts for Ladies (*c.* 1850).

Reports of the Juries and Catalogue of the Exhibition . . . 1851.

Caplin, Madame, *Health and Beauty, or Corsets and Clothing* (*c.* 1855).

The What-Not or Ladies' Handbook, 1862.

A Manual of Needlework, 1873.

The Lady's Knitting Book, 1879.

How to Dress Well on a Shilling a Day, by Sylvia (*c.* 1875).

Ballin, Ada S. *Science of Dress in Theory and Practice*, 1885.

Giles, E. B. *History of the Art of Cutting in England*, 1887.

Davis, J. E. *Elements of Modern Dressmaking*, 1896.

Clothes and the Man, by "The Major", 1900.

MODERN WRITINGS:

Laver, James. *Taste and Fashion from the French Revolution to the Present Day*, 1937.

Cunnington, C. Willett. *Englishwomen's Clothing in the Nineteenth Century*, 1937.

Cunnington, C. Willett (with Phillis Cunnington). *The History of Underclothes*, 1951; *Handbook of English Costume in the Nineteenth Century*, 1959.

Davenport, Millia. *The Book of Costume*, 1948.

Moore, Doris Langley. *The Woman in Fashion*, 1949; *The Child in Fashion*, 1953.

Libron, F., and Clouzet, H. *Le Corset dans l'Art*, 1933.

Waugh, Norah. *Corsets and Crinolines*, 1954.

Blair, M. *The Paisley Shawl*, 1904.

Dony, J. G. *A History of the Straw Hat Industry*, 1942.

Rhead, G. Woolliscroft. *History of the Fan*, 1910.

Flower, Margaret. *Victorian Jewellery*, 1951.

Holland, V. *Handcoloured Fashion Plates, 1770–1899*, 1955.

MUSEUM PUBLICATIONS:

Victoria and Albert Museum: *Costume Illustration: The Nineteenth Century*, 1947; Irwin, John. *Shawls*, 1955.

London Museum: *Catalogue: Costume*, 1935.

Manchester City Art Galleries, Gallery of English Costume: *Women's Costume, 1835–70*, 1951; *Women's Costume, 1870–1900*, 1955; *Children's Costume, 1800–1900*, 1959.

Luton Museum: *Luton and the Hat Industry*, 1953.

ADDITIONS TO BIBLIOGRAPHY

Adburgham, A. *A Punch History of Modes and Manners 1840–1940*, 1961; *Shops and Shopping 1800–1914*, 1964, n.e. 1981

Armstrong, N. *A Collector's History of Fans*, 1974

Arnold, J. *Patterns of Fashion I 1660–1860, II 1860–1940*, 1972

Byrde, P. *The Male Image. Men's Fashion in Britain 1300–1970*, 1979

Clabburn, P. *Shawls in Imitation of the Indian*, 1981

Clark, F. *Hats. (Costume Accessories Series)*, 1982

Cumming, V. *Gloves. (Costume Accessories Series)*, 1982

Cunnington, C.W. and P. *History of Underclothes*, n.e. revised by A. and V. Mansfield, 1981

Cunnington, P. and Buck, A. *Children's Costume in England from the Fifteenth to the end of the Nineteenth Century*, 1965

Ewing, E. *Fashion in Underwear*, 1971, n.e. *Dress and Undress*, 1978; *History of Children's Costume*, 1977

Foster, V. *Bags and Purses. (Costume Accessories Series)*, 1982; *The Nineteenth Century. (A Visual History of Costume Series)*, 1984

Gernsheim, A. *Fashion and Reality 1840–1914*, 1963

Ginsburg, M. *Victorian Dress in Photographs*, 1982

Hinks, P. *Nineteenth Century Jewellery*, 1975

de Marly, D. *The History of Haute Couture*, 1980; *Worth, Father of Haute Couture*, 1980

Mayor, S. *Collecting Fans*, 1980

Moore, D. L. *Fashion Through Fashion Plates 1771–1970*, 1971

Newton, S. M. *Health, Art and Reason. Dress Reformers of the Nineteenth Century*, 1974

Swann, J. *Shoes. (Costume Accessories Series)*, 1982

Walkley, C. *The Ghost in the Looking Glass. The Victorian Seamstress*, 1981

Walkley, C. and Foster, V. *Crinolines and Crimping Irons. Victorian Clothes – how they were cleaned and cared for*, 1978

Waugh, N. *The Cut of Men's Clothes 1600–1900*, 1964; *The Cut of Women's Clothes 1600–1930*, 1968

Costume Society Articles in *Costume*, the Journal of the Society 1967– , also conference papers, *Early Victorian 1830–60* (1969), *High Victorian 1860–90* (1968), *La Belle Epoque 1890–1914* (1967)

MUSEUM PUBLICATIONS:

Leicestershire Museums: Page, C. *Foundation of Fashion. The Symington Collection of Corsetry from 1856 to the Present Day*, 1981

Liverpool, Merseyside Museums: Jarvis, A. *Liverpool Fashion: its makers and wearers. The dressmaking trade in Liverpool 1831–1940*, 1981

Paisley Museum and Art Gallery: Rock, C.H. *Paisley Shawls*, 1966

Royal Scottish Museum: Tarrant, N. *The Rise and Fall of the Sleeve 1825–1840*, 1983

Worthing Museum and Art Gallery: Clark, F. *Costume in Worthing Museum*, 1981

INDEX

References to parts of dress, e.g. bodice, skirt, neckline, collar, etc., which form part of the descriptions of each style and recur several times in each section dealing with dresses, are not given in the index, unless they separate accessories or have a particular emphasis.